PRAISE
THE WILD WO

"*The Wild Woman's Way* drips from the [...] As pragmatic as it is compassionate, [...] mately relaxing invitation to re-wild yourself, stripping away all that is not your true nature, will leave you inspired and curious to discover the wild woman within."

—Lissa Rankin, MD, *New York Times* bestselling author of *Mind Over Medicine*

"I love this book. Herein lie simple beautiful secrets to being kinder to yourself, making you and those around you happier, healthier, and more fulfilled. Being a wild woman sounds wildly wonderful."

—Chris Martin, singer-songwriter, Coldplay

"A concentrated dose of playful wisdom about the realms of energy, connection, and love! Much needed in this wild world of ours!"

—Jesse Carmichael, Maroon 5

"Let Michaela's wisdom lead you to a new, harmonious relationship with your body, your beloved, and your boss. From outer work to inner sensuality, *The Wild Woman's Way* is an essential guide to learning how to find your 'flow.'"

—HeatherAsh Amara, author of *Warrior Goddess Training*

"*The Wild Woman's Way* is a road map to living your life with sensuality and strength; you will gain more power and joy as these pages reawaken your inner wild woman who has been waiting to be expressed."

—Christy Whitman, *New York Times* bestselling author of *The Art of Having It All* and *Quantum Success*

"Through simple, thoughtful exercises and engaging personal and client stories, Michaela Boehm invites us into the dancing heart of our own lusciousness, and teaches us how to share it with others. I think this book should be a required manual for all women—to live the lives we were born to in all of our capacities, and with joy and purpose."

—Rachel Carlton Abrams, MD, coauthor of *The Multi-Orgasmic Woman*

"Wise, warm, and wonderful, like sitting around the fire, listening to stories from a brave adventurer in the inner worlds."

—Lorin Roche, PhD, author of *The Radiance Sutras*

"Michaela Boehm is, in my opinion, the most advanced teacher currently sharing wisdom about the intersection of sexuality and spirituality. *The Wild Woman's Way* is Michaela's kindhearted and clear-headed encapsulation of a foundational area within her vast knowledge. May this fabulous and long-awaited debut book—which everyone with a body should read—be the first in a library of her teachings."

—Michael Ellsberg, author of *The Education of Millionaires*

"Listen. Let go. Live. The invitation back home to your wild, natural self lies within these pages, immersed in the embodied wisdom of one who walks her talk. Read. Relax. Reclaim what has always been yours."

—Saida Désilets, PhD, author of *Emergence of the Sensual Woman*

"A must-read for every Goddess looking to dial up the way they woman. The wild. The raw. The wise. Michaela Boehm walks you through every ounce of womanhood in these beautifully honest pages that are sure to find you unlocking your inner power and pleasure centers."

—Emma Mildon, bestselling author of *The Soul Searcher's Handbook* and *Evolution of Goddess*

"Every page reveals the sacred wisdom of how to fully embody the divine pleasure of life."

—Rikka Zimmerman, creator of Life Transformed™ and singer-songwriter

"The most practical and inspiring guide yet to self-care for a woman's physical, spiritual, and emotional needs."

—Debbie Phillips, founder and CEO of Women on Fire

THE
Wild
WOMAN'S WAY

Reconnect to
Your Body's Wisdom

MICHAELA BOEHM

ENLIVEN BOOKS
—
ATRIA

New York London Toronto Sydney New Delhi

ENLIVEN
ATRIA

An Imprint of Simon & Schuster, Inc.
1230 Avenue of the Americas
New York, NY 10020

First Enliven Books/Atria Paperback edition November 2021

This publication contains the opinions and ideas of its author. It is intended to provide
helpful and informative material on the subjects addressed in the publication. It is sold with
the understanding that the author and publisher are not engaged in rendering medical, health,
or any other kind of personal professional services in the book.
The reader should consult his or her medical, health, or other competent professional
before adopting any of the suggestions in this book or drawing inferences from it.

The author and publisher specifically disclaim all responsibility for any liability, loss, or risk,
personal or otherwise, which is incurred as a consequence, directly or indirectly,
of the use and application of any of the contents of this book.

For information about special discounts for bulk purchases, please contact
Simon & Schuster Special Sales at 1-866-506-1949 or business@simonandschuster.com.

The Simon & Schuster Speakers Bureau can bring authors to your live event. For more
information or to book an event, contact the Simon & Schuster Speakers Bureau at
1-866-248-3049 or visit our website at www.simonspeakers.com.

Interior design by Amy Trombat

Manufactured in the United States of America

3   5   7   9   10   8   6   4

Library of Congress Cataloging-in-Publication Data

Names: Boehm, Michaela, author.
Title: The wild woman's way: unlock your full potential for pleasure, power,
and fulfillment / Michaela Boehm.
Description: First Enliven Books hardcover edition. | New York:
Atria/Enliven Books, 2018.
Identifiers: LCCN 2018010213 (print) | LCCN 2018018569 (ebook) | ISBN
9781501179907 (eBook) | ISBN 9781501179884 (hardback) | ISBN 9781501179891 (paperback)
Subjects: LCSH: Self-actualization (Psychology) | Mind and body. | Tantrism.
| Happiness. | Women—Psychology. | BISAC: SELF-HELP / Personal Growth /
Happiness. | BODY, MIND & SPIRIT / Inspiration & Personal Growth. | FAMILY
& RELATIONSHIPS / Love & Romance.
Classification: LCC BF637.S4 (ebook) | LCC BF637.S4 B624 2018 (print) | DDC
155.3/339—dc23
LC record available at https://lccn.loc.gov/2018010213

ISBN 978-1-5011-7988-4
ISBN 978-1-5011-7989-1 (pbk)
ISBN 978-1-5011-7990-7 (ebook)

For my parents, Sylvia and Ulrich

Contents

INTRODUCTION *1*

I. GOING BACK TO NATURE *13*

1. The Wild Woman *15*
2. The Plight of the Modern Woman *25*
3. Women and the Feminine *35*
4. Re-wilding the Feminine *45*

II. A WOMAN'S FEELING BODY *57*

5. Energetics in a Woman's Body *59*
6. Embodiment *71*
7. Barriers to Embodiment *83*
8. Intuition *99*
9. Pleasure Is Our Birthright *113*
10. Orgasm *131*
11. The Wise Woman *139*

III. THE UNTAMED HEART *149*

12. Dating *151*
13. Relationships *159*
14. Tribe *173*
15. Career *183*
16. Children *191*

IV. SACRED PRACTICES OF THE WILD WOMAN *197*

A Note on Practice *199*

1. *The Wild Woman's Foundational Practice 201*
2. *Embodiment and Aliveness 202*
3. *Relaxation 205*
4. *Re-sensitizing 207*

5. *Movement 209*

6. *Expanding Your Repertoire 214*

7. *Rituals 217*

8. *Altars and Beauty 224*

9. *Communion with Nature 227*

10. *Animals 231*

11. *Creativity 232*

12. *Sensuality Hacks 235*

V. CLOSING *237*

ACKNOWLEDGMENTS *239*

RESOURCES *241*

BIBLIOGRAPHY *243*

NOTES *244*

THE
Wild
WOMAN'S WAY

Introduction

THIS BOOK IS FIRST AND FOREMOST MY PASSIONATE LOVE LETTER TO the body: an invitation for each of us to remember the innate wisdom of our bodies—not our looks, or our various shapes and sizes, but the living, feeling body as a portal to unlocking who we truly are.

Our bodily genius is a premier decision-making tool, a navigation device extraordinaire, an agent of release and healing, a wisdom-carrier of deep insight, and a holder of secrets and mysteries.

This book is a call to come back to our wild, undomesticated "original nature," which, combined with an untamed heart, knows what is true for each of us. It is a call to return to the inborn genius that guides our passion, whispers in our ear with longing, and reveals itself abundantly when we allow our bodies to show us the way.

This is a deeply personal book, born from my own explorations, struggles, and victories, infused with my passion carried over the span of more than twenty years of teaching and mentoring individuals and couples in the realms of relationship and sexuality.

I am focusing here on women's bodies, for a few reasons.

First, I am happily living in a woman's body—yes, I said happily!—and as such am continually traversing both the fertile lands of feeling embodiment and the turbulent seas of unfeeling numbness. I am also the lineage holder, a keeper and teacher of the ancient wisdom of a Kashmiri Tantric tradition that has been passed down from woman to woman for thousands of years, and, as such, am dedicated to empowering women's understanding of their bodies as a devotional vehicle. I see the current cultural emergence of the sacred feminine as a beautiful opportunity for exploration and growth, and, at the same time, a movement fraught with the dangers of gender wars and false entitlement.

I am writing this book mainly for women. I also hope that men will benefit: in their relationship with their own bodies, and by gaining a different access to and understanding about what it is like to be a woman in the twenty-first century.

I personally love men, and am fortunate to be surrounded by wonderful, talented men with generous hearts. This is not a book to set men against women and fuel a battle of the sexes; it is instead an exploration of what defines us as men and women, what unites us, and how to become whole and serve one another as we traverse these extraordinary times.

Never have we as women in the West had more opportunity, more choice, and more freedom. Granted, we still have a long way to go, yet compared to any other time in history, we have the greatest options and choices to forge our own paths and determine our own destinies. At the same time, with these opportunities come new challenges and distinct difficulties: the demands of life have created unprecedented levels of stress, pressure, disconnect, discomfort, and dis-ease in women.

We women are now, more than ever, able to have the careers we want, whether that is to be an entrepreneur, a CEO, a full-time parent, an educator, or a social media sensation. We make our own money and our own decisions. We vote, we march, and we support our causes. We have more freedom today than ever before to determine the kind of relationships we want—and freedom to determine if, and how, we will birth and raise children, and to make decisions about how our households will be taken care of.

With all these options, there are a dizzying variety of versions of "Woman" to which we can aspire: Boardroom Executive, Mother, Entrepreneur, Martha-Stewart-like Homemaker, Vixen in the Bedroom, Visionary, Academic, Artist, Yogini, Leader, Goddess, Scientist, Earth Mother, Warrior. We are told we should "lean in," "drop out," and, on top of it all, "be forever young and radiant."

Then there are the spiritual choices. We can practice yoga, chant, dance ecstatically, meditate in a vast variety of traditions, go Zen, swirl like a Sufi, discover the Goddess or reclaim God, take "plant medicines," and embrace a variety of pagan traditions. We can follow one teacher, or piece all the above together into our own á la carte menu of spirituality.

We can even combine our quests of spirit and sex through a variety of Tantric explorations. The options to work on our feminine wiles have vastly increased, from wrapping ourselves around a stripper pole, to "vajazzling" our previously private parts, to sex-toy parties and hands-on classes on how to achieve multiple orgasms.

Regardless of what we choose (and regardless of how tired we are), we are also women who want meaningful relationships and fulfilling sex lives, with all their inherent benefits and responsibilities.

The good news: amidst such a multitude of options we are free to choose what resonates with us. The bad news: it's confusing, overwhelming, time-consuming, fraught with many pitfalls, and requires constant discernment.

No wonder we often find ourselves confused, stressed, and unsure of what to do and how to be. Even though there are abundant choices, there are subtle (and sometimes not-so-subtle) pressures from society, spiritual and communal dogma, our own belief systems, and the habit patterns of our past that tell us that we have to be Superwoman to be loved, or that our real choices are narrower than we thought them to be.

More than ever, it's time for each of us to ask ourselves:

Who am I out in the world?
Who am I when no one is watching?
What does my unguarded heart yearn for?
Who am I when everything is stripped away?
How does my body want to move when I am alone?
What would I do if nothing was required of me?

These are the kinds of questions I ask women in my workshops. When they hear them for the first time, their initial response is almost always stunned silence.

Within the swirl of all the demands and options of a busy life, it becomes hard to know who we are, and almost impossible to discern what our best choices are.

In the midst of this paradox of opportunity and confusion, we have become disconnected from our most valuable ally: our body.

Stress, tension, overwhelm, and excess mental activity are drowning out our feeling. We no longer notice our bodily sensations or our emotions as they attempt to arise within our being. Without access to the subtle genius of our feeling body, we have a reduced ability to discern and respond accurately.

Thankfully, the way out of this conundrum is neither time-consuming nor expensive, and it is within the reach of every woman, no matter her schedule and commitments. In fact, the process of reconnecting with our bodily genius is something profoundly natural to every woman.

The solution lies not in adding to or enhancing our bodies, or chasing after some external ideal; it lies in remembering that the body is not just a vehicle that needs to be maintained (or disciplined) so that we can function; rather, it is a potent source of power, intuition, feeling, and abundant pleasure.

Feeling is our birthright. It is innate wisdom, and through reconnecting with it, we can re-wild ourselves back to our original nature: the place we started from, before layers of doing, pushing, and obligation clouded over who we are.

> Feeling is our birthright. It is innate wisdom, and through reconnecting with it, we can re-wild ourselves back to our original nature: the place we started from, before layers of doing, pushing, and obligation clouded over who we are.

In this book, I share the lessons I learned myself, not only over years of building a career while maintaining a marriage but also from a lifetime of commitment to and exploration in the creative and spiritual inner life. These, together with my Tantric training, and my many years of giving workshops and client sessions, form the basis for the exercises and teachings presented in each chapter.

Working with this book, you will gain understanding of the challenges that are unique to women at this moment, as well as the mechanics that drive our bodies and minds.

You will receive information and practices to help you re-sensitize yourself and come back to your body.

By reconnecting with your feeling body, you will begin to allow its innate wisdom to inform you. As you rediscover instinct, intuition, and power, you will gain the discernment to make decisions that honor your own true nature, as well as that of others.

From there, we will explore what you are devoted to—your passion, purpose, and heart's yearning—so that you can infuse your career, your relationships, and your creative and spiritual life with your deepest meaning.

And then, once your body and heart have reconnected, we'll explore your relationship to sensual and sexual pleasure within yourself, and as an offering to the partner of your choice.

The practices in this book are easy to incorporate into your life. They don't require big changes or great time commitments. They are designed to gradually integrate what is important to you into your existing routine. They allow you to shift and explore gently, from the inside out, infusing everything you do with who you are at your very core: the wild, untamed, undomesticated, embodied self that has always been there.

My Journey

When I was twelve, I decided to become a witch. Not that I really knew what that meant, but I had very strong ideas nonetheless. I was going to have a house in the country, with lots of animals and a large kitchen garden. I envisioned people coming to receive potions and spells. I could see it clearly and had distinct ideas of what I would do to empower and heal the women coming to my door.

My father's godfather gifted me a copy of *The Mists of Avalon* for my twelfth birthday. I was a voracious reader, and finished the book in record time. I read about priestesses, sorceresses, and powerful women, about the mother lineage, gods and goddesses uniting in ritual for the sake of the land (not that, as a twelve-year-old, I had any idea what that really meant, either).

This book introduced me to the concepts of nondualism and reincarnation, which, strangely, to my twelve-year-old self, made perfect sense. I was determined to learn about herb lore, water magic, and how to grow and harvest healing herbs in concert with the moon. As far as I was concerned, my career path was clear.

I grew up in a rural part of Austria, an area made famous to filmgoers as the meadows that Julie Andrews skipped upon in *The Sound of Music*. This part of Austria was still connected to its Celtic roots, so it was easy for me to immerse myself in the rituals and teachings of working with the moon and elements. A local woman named Magdalena introduced me to Celtic biodynamic practices and herb lore.

I was educated in an all-girls school, which, at the time, caused me great upset; yet in hindsight, I can't thank my parents enough. Educated in this way, I had no sense of girls being less than boys, or of women being discriminated against or uneducated.

On the contrary, I was schooled with rigor and academic excellence in a curriculum that was both heavy on science and also had all the teachings of a finishing school. My schoolmates and I were taught how to cook, sew, and knit, and at the same time, to speak three languages, translate Caesar's *Bellum Gallicum,* and to explore black holes and red dwarfs, as well as career skills in the modern working world. When I was sixteen, I had to spend two weeks during summer holidays apprenticing at a hospital, in the delivery and newborn ward (an experience that proved to be a better contraceptive than any parental talk ever could have been!).

In this educational environment, I had no idea that there was such a thing as "the patriarchy," and grew up with a sense of possibility, and the confidence that I could do anything I wanted.

When I was in my mid-teens, the herb woman, Magdalena, introduced me to a friend of hers, an Indian woman named Deepa who was skilled in Ayurveda and potion-making, and I eagerly began to study with her. She became my mentor and teacher.

My time was divided between school, tending and riding horses, and learning about the mysteries of spices, teas, sound, and movement from my teacher. For the first few years, all I learned from my teacher was how to make chai, by tasting, working with, and combining each ingredient at length. I also swept, and swept, and swept some more around a very leafy tree in her courtyard; the ground around it had to be clean at all times for the chalk paintings she drew each day as a meditative practice.

Over time, it became clear to me that there was more to this woman than chai tea and chalk paintings. As I began to pass tests of concentration, commitment, and consistency that were woven into these initial practices, she began to invite me deeper into the knowledge that she carried and practiced.

Chai-making gave way to the secret practices of her lineage, and it soon became clear that this unusual woman was in fact a true Tantrika, a stealth householder who shared her knowledge only when it could be received. She was the very embodiment of both deep mystery and the sacred ordinary.

Many of the lessons and skills she taught me in those years form the basis of my teaching and my life today. It was only much later that I realized the wisdom behind her insistence on keeping things in her particular way. By having me repeat seemingly boring, mundane tasks over and over, she instilled in me focus, concentration, and discipline, all things that by no means came naturally to me. Only when I had integrated these lessons was I ready for the deeper teachings: the teachings of the wisdom of the body.

Over the years, as I continued to study with my teacher, I pursued an education in psychology and worked at a variety of jobs. I moved twice to follow my teacher when she moved to different cities in Germany. From those first chai lessons in my mid-teens until I was twenty-eight, I dedicated myself body and soul to the ancient lineage of women into which I had been invited.

Then, through a series of twists and turns, I moved to Los Angeles. In the beginning, I worked a full-time day job while building a private counseling practice in the evenings. Somewhere along the way, I forgot about the pursuit of "witchy" and magical things and instead became a businesswoman. I often spent twelve to fourteen hours a day working, splitting my time between the actual counseling work I was passionate about and the endless loop of booking clients, getting new ones, keeping on top of paperwork, and managing my practice.

Over the years, I built a wildly successful full-time counseling practice and began working with celebrities, entertainers, high-performers, and family offices.

When I met my future husband, I realized that my driven, hardworking, goal-oriented consultant persona got in the way of enjoying my personal life. I was no longer able to switch out of "go" mode easily, and it took some work (and struggle) to reconcile the various parts of me. Searching for balance, I began to remember the practices I had been taught, and started a women's circle in the garage of my house.

The circle met twice a month, and the connection with the other women in the group became an important part of my life. We were all exploring the same themes: having a career, and wanting a fulfilling relationship and time for self-expression, yet feeling stuck in achieving those goals. Realizing this, I began to experiment with different modalities for each group meeting. We would share what happened during our week, connect with ourselves and one another, and then move our bodies to release tension and stress. Over time, the movement exercises reconnected us to the untamed and sensual parts of ourselves, and gave us access to a whole different kind of wisdom. These early explorations eventually led to the development of the Non-Linear Movement Method®, a transformative and awakening somatic movement technique that has helped many women awaken their wise, wild selves, and which I will share with you in this book.

As my relationship with my partner progressed and we married, all the different parts of me were still at war, and it took a few years to integrate them and come to terms with my complex inner life. It was confusing, with various and sometimes contradictory advice and teachings competing in my head.

I had to come to terms with the fact that I actually enjoyed being in charge of my own business and my money—and that I was really good at it! No amount of hearing that I was "too much in my masculine energy" or "not feminine enough" would change that.

I also came to understand that, at the same time, I had a deep yearning for union, both with my husband and in the spiritual sense of union with the divine, and with my own divine nature. I wanted a full-on, committed relationship but I also wanted to have freedom and the ability to spend time alone. My marriage became the testing ground for all the things I had taught people during my counseling years, as well as for the practices of my emerging workshop teachings.

At some point, the reach of these offerings expanded, and I was teaching workshops and taking on new clients in Europe, which meant nearly constant travel and substantial stress. My clients in England lived on a sublime piece of property, with gardens, fields, and large trees. During breaks, I would sit out in the flower garden and immerse myself in the beauty of nature while dealing with my almost constant jet lag.

Slowly, over the course of several visits, my connection with the English countryside grew, opening my memory of my upbringing, and my connection with Celtic magic lore and the rhythms of the land. I began to envision having a piece of earth of my own. I spent many of my transcontinental flights imagining that land and feeling it in my body, planning what flowers and herbs I would grow, which animals I would have, and what I could do on my own property.

Within that year, through a series of miraculous events (which included getting the last "no-doc" loan before the housing crash), I managed to buy a beautiful four-acre piece of land outside of Ojai, California.

I built my own teaching studio, planted a full herb and vegetable garden, and filled the place with rescued animals. Working on my land reconnected me to myself. I started to gradually remember all that had been taught to me by my parents and teachers, and my passion for nature and animals.

I began attending to my marriage and my personal life from the place in me that was connected to my "original nature." Over time, relationships and business that were not aligned with this essential part of me fell away, and other opportunities opened. I began teaching differently in my workshops, letting my practices, the land, and my experience inform the lessons, and the way I approached them.

At home, surrounded with what was dear to me, even when I was spending eight hours a day answering e-mails, I could smell a home-grown rose or cuddle one of my dogs and draw inspiration and endless creative energy from the interaction.

After I received the lineage from Deepa, before she died, my teaching took on a different orientation, and a new creativity and urgency infused my life. I now feel a strong passion for adapting the ancient practices I received so that they can fit into our hectic modern lifestyle.

And one day recently, while I sat on the patio swing waiting for my workshop participants to arrive, I realized that thirty years later, I had ended up with exactly what I had envisioned as a girl: a place in the country, with gardens and animals, where people could come to heal and learn. Like my teacher before me, I had created a place from which I could share the fruits of my own learning and life experience.

Your Journey

Each of us has that native, embodied wisdom—a wild, untamed, un-domesticated body-mind and heart that knows what is true for us. This looks and feels different for each woman, and no two are ever alike. It guides our passion, whispers in our ears with longing, and reveals itself when we allow the natural genius of our bodies to show us the way.

> Each of us has that native, embodied wisdom—a wild, untamed, undomesticated body-mind and heart that knows what is true for us. This looks and feels different for each woman, and no two are ever alike. It guides our passion, whispers in our ears with longing, and reveals itself when we allow the natural genius of our bodies to show us the way.

I am so excited to share these past thirty years of my own ongoing exploration, experience, practice, teaching of and research into this deeply connected and embodied lifestyle with you, so that you can find what is true for you, and infuse your life with your very own embodied wisdom.

This book is an invitation to re-wild yourself, to strip away layers of

coping, adaptation, and trauma to reveal what has always been there—
what is ready to emerge, free from internal and external beliefs and dogma.

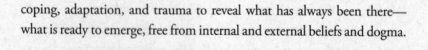

> This book is an invitation to re-wild yourself, to strip
> away layers of coping, adaptation, and trauma to reveal
> what has always been there—what is ready to emerge,
> free from internal and external beliefs and dogma.

This is not a book to help you learn yet another set of ways to be "more feminine" or a collection of tricks that, when applied, will make you "good enough." This is a collection of real pieces of wisdom, honest stories, and powerful exercises that I offer to you—as they were once offered to me—which have been pivotal in transforming the lives of countless women who have participated in my workshops and sessions, and can do the same for you. This book's purpose is to empower you, to reveal your feminine birthright, allowing you to find the passion, purpose, and pleasure that are intimately connected to who *you* really are.

I

Going Back to Nature

1

The Wild Woman

SO, WHO IS THE WILD WOMAN, YOU ASK? BEING THE WILD WOMAN sounds alluring and impossible, dangerous and maybe a little bit crazy. Often, when I teach a Wild Woman's Way Intensive at the Esalen Institute, curious participants from other workshops come by our dining tables or even peek at us in the workshop hall. "Oh, so you are the Wild Women," they say—the women often with a glint in their eyes, the men sometimes a bit hesitantly. They might admit with a grin that they expected to see crazed, wild-haired creatures, foaming at their fanged mouths and clawing the walls. Amidst the laughter of these curious people, you can often see yearning, intrigue, or repulsion in their eyes.

The women in the course usually laugh and play it up a bit, giving mysterious answers and enjoying the attention. Some of them are not yet quite sure who this Wild Woman within themselves is.

The Wild Woman is a part of each of us. She is not the crazed and uncivilized creature she is sometimes made out to be, but the part of us that is deeply and inextricably connected to natural life; she is the ancient part of us that knows of the rising of the moon and the movement of the tides, the instinctual, deeply connected aspect in each of us that has survived and thrived in the wilderness for many thousands of years.

She embodies knowledge of curing and healing, ritual and prayer; of the tracker, hunter, gatherer, and shaman. She is connected to all things in nature, including her own body, whom she cares for and utilizes as an instrument of perception. She represents the part of each woman that comes from nature and is part of nature.

The Wild Woman is an archetype, and as such, can rise from the unconscious and come into play when the time is right. She is a portal to natural empowerment, through which we understand that we don't have to "become someone else" to be loved, that who we are is utterly perfect, and that each of us is born with a natural genius that can be revealed and will bloom with the help of our body's native intelligence.

Archetypes were brought to wider awareness by the Swiss psychiatrist and psychoanalyst Carl Jung. He understood archetypes as universal, ancient images and patterns that arise from the collective unconscious. Because they are unconscious, they have to be brought to light and awareness through examining art, imagery, myths, dreams, and human behavior.

Myths, stories, and fairy tales are subconscious archetypal material already modified to be brought into the conscious as a means of transmission and teaching. They exist in every tradition, and we find the same themes recurring in them, regardless of the culture or religion to which they are connected.

Each archetype holds the collective power and knowledge that resides in all of us, and working with an archetype can awaken the attributes and wisdom innate in each individual.

As Carl Jung wrote, "In each of these images there is a little piece of human psychology and human fate, a remnant of the joys and sorrows that have been repeated countless times in our ancestral history." [1]

The archetype of the Wild Woman beckons us to "come back to nature"—our nature.

The archetype of the Wild Woman beckons us
to "come back to nature"—our nature.

What this means on a practical level—and what we'll explore in this book—is stripping away the layers of stress, muscle clench, coping, and other related habits to reveal our deeper nature, the discovery and reclamation of the innate knowledge our body holds, reconnecting to our nature, our rhythms, and our unique gifts.

It means relaxing the internal push so we connect to our native cycles, not only hormonally but also in all aspects of life. It means finding *our* way to eat and sleep, and who we connect with and how we move. It means discovering who we are when all the "should's" and "have-to's" are stripped away, and how we express when we don't strive to be someone we are not meant to be.

The Wild Woman is the antidote to the common self-development fallacy, which operates on "not being enough." By taking yet another course, yet another coaching session, yet another kind of yoga-meditation-exercise-diet program, we believe we will finally achieve what it takes to be loved, successful, and "enough."

The Wild Woman is the antidote to the common self-development
fallacy, which operates on "not being enough." By taking yet
another course, yet another coaching session, yet another kind of
yoga-meditation-exercise-diet program, we believe we will finally
achieve what it takes to be loved, successful, and "enough."

Media, advertising, society, and often our upbringing make us believe that we are lacking. We change our behavior to get the love and
support of those who raise us and often lose our individuality for the
sake of fitting into the construct of society and family.

Not being enough is big business. It sells us so much of what we
don't really need; and it is an endless project that keeps us numb to
what we really feel. There is always something else to strive for, and that
striving temporarily overrides the feelings of inadequacy. We strive so
hard to be whatever success and love mean to us that we forget that who
we are is just fine—that who we are is unique, precious, and inimitable.

I'm not saying that you should not learn new skills or develop yourself; I'm saying that you don't need to do it from a place of lack. There is
a fundamental difference between trying to change to get love, money,
fame, looks, etc. (fill in the blank here) in order to feel adequate, and
seeing yourself as perfect and complete as a human being, and from
there acquiring whatever skills or adjustments are wanted or needed.

Coming from a place of abundance versus a feeling of lack changes
everything. When we appreciate our body as the vehicle that allows us
to be alive, moving and living in this world, it is much easier to care for
it, knowing that by doing so, we serve it better. When you think your
body-mind is not what it should be, you are inflicting punishment on it
to try to make it become what you want it to be.

When you truly care for your body, the actions you take might look
the same, but the sentiments behind them are very different. Coming
back to who we are, connecting with our body's wisdom, our spirit's
determination, and our natural intelligence, we tie back in to what has
been available to us for millions of years. We access the "World Wide
Web" of the natural world, with more information and wisdom available than we could ever acquire by ourselves.

Through relaxation and sensitization, we connect to our body of
knowledge. And in turn, who we are can unfold, and our unique gifts
be given and shown. It's not just about being with nature, though, but
also being connected to instincts, cultivating a strong decision-making

capacity, and trusting ourselves, each of us expressing as the unique and beautiful flavor that we are.

The Wild Woman is not a fixed idea or a template into which we need to fit ourselves, but rather a portal, an entry point into a vast and rich inner landscape.

> **The Wild Woman is not a fixed idea or a template into which we need to fit ourselves, but rather a portal, an entry point into a vast and rich inner landscape.**

In my workshops, we begin with story and myth, to help unearth each woman's individual expression of the Wild Woman archetype. From there, we intersperse various talk processes to cognitively clarify the Wild Woman, along with embodiment practices and movement to facilitate her expression via the body. We use art, ritual, and music to deepen the investigation.

Every workshop takes a different form, since each woman has a unique exploration with the Wild Woman. No two women are alike, and hence, no two expressions are the same. At some point in the workshop, each woman gets up to move and be witnessed in the myth she created and the archetype she is expressing.

It is always touching, surprising, and inspiring to see what presents itself. Witnessing the unfolding is both instructional for the viewer and deeply empowering for the woman expressing herself.

In my work, bodily engagement and embodiment practices are the key to accessing and subsequently integrating any learning. It is important not only to cognitively entertain ourselves, but also to let the body access, understand, and express who we are.

The work is not about going back to nature in a world-denying, granola-crunching, unwashed-and-ungroomed kind of way, but rather about integrating ancient wisdom, the natural genius of our bodies, and the many opportunities available to us now. The aim is to empower the deepest expression of each person in the context of a truly meaningful life.

To me, the Wild Woman is really an access point, a place from which to start and discover who we are. Discovering our body's wisdom takes a very different approach than understanding something cognitively. Despite our best attempts, we cannot think our way into feeling and perceiving from the depth of our body's knowing. Engaging with an archetype helps us to access a shared, deeper knowing that facilitates the body's awakening.

The archetype can take on many forms. You might feel that the Wild Woman expresses as Mother, Wise Woman, Wrathful Woman, Warrior Woman, Healer, and/or Destroyer, as needed. The power and knowledge of these collective energies becomes available through the genius of the body. In the body, we each carry instinctive information that is far deeper than what we can conceive of in our minds. By engaging with the stories and images of archetypes, we invoke the lived experience of all women before us and connect ourselves to the deeper collective wisdom.

Women's bodies learn through resonance. By connecting with the positive attributes of an archetype, we invoke those parts in us naturally. When the movie *Wonder Woman* was released, many women reported that they left the theater feeling powerful in their bodies, infused with feminine strength. In the same way, we can invoke our collective experiences powerfully in our bodies through the Wild Woman archetype.

. . . .

Women's bodies learn through resonance. By connecting with the positive attributes of an archetype, we invoke those parts in us naturally.

. . . .

Exercise to Connect with Your Wild Woman Archetypes

For a moment, consider female characters that you are drawn to, either in myths, books, or movies. Let yourself imagine and feel their most powerful attributes and notice what happens in your body and mood. The attributes that light you up the most will support you to awaken your unique expression of the Wild Woman. As you go through your day, look for examples of those attributes in yourself and other women.

My work was born from the desire to explore and share the wider considerations of living life as a woman in the twenty-first century. We live in an unprecedented time, with incredible technology and opportunity. At the same time, we are more disconnected from nature and our own natural expression than ever before. Through the lens of the Wild Woman, we can engage with sustainable, integrated ways to have a career, a relationship, and if we choose, a family, and to deepen our pleasure, intuition, and creativity.

This book is meant to be a practical tool, and presents a multitude of exercises. It is also meant to provide food for thought and inspiration for your own explorations. My wish is to give you a "how-to manual" of a different kind, one that does not tell you what to do "cookie-cutter style," but instead facilitates your unique form of empowered, embodied living with the help of your body's wisdom.

My interests in myth and archetype really started back when, at twelve, I read *The Mists of Avalon*. The stories in the book had a visceral effect on my being. I had always felt strongly about connecting with nature, especially with animals. My very first mentor, the herbal healer Magdalena, taught me about plants, tracking the stars, the weather, and how to perceive the seasons.

In the Celtic-Catholic traditions of my home country, the saints and Mother Mary are the portals through which wisdom and compassion are transmitted. Magdalena wove many of the stories about them into our time together and connected them with the herb lore and the creation of remedies.

In the part of Austria where I grew up, statues and roadside shrines can be found on every path, and most farmhouses have a small chapel. Even though the archetypal engagement is somewhat tinged with religious dogma, it gives symbolic meaning to life.

My first formal engagement with archetypal work came from my main teacher, Deepa, the woman who trained me in the lineage of Kashmiri Shaivism I now hold. She instructed me via the archetypes of that lineage. My first practical engagement with the archetype of the Wild Woman came in the form of Kali, the Hindu goddess of destruction and rebirth.

Kali, more than any other representation of the Wild Woman, has the fierce and physically wild expression that people often imagine when first hearing about the Wild Woman archetype. Her wildness does not come from anger or crazed frenzy; it comes from an immediate response to circumstances, and is born from deep love. She destroys whatever is less than love, so more love can be born. Her instincts and responses are immediate because they spring from her deep connection to her nature and her state of being fully present to each moment.

After Kali came many different forms of the Wild Woman. Her youthful form of Lalita, the goddess of desire, her abundant beauty as Lakshmi, her artistic form as Saraswati the muse, and her old crone form as Dhumavati the widow. I worked with all of these forms and more under my teacher's guidance. Access to those archetypes came via rigorous bodily instruction, given so I could feel, perceive, and intuit with the entirety of my being, using the yogic techniques of devotion and merging that weave these practices into every layer of one's being. This is the practice of Deity Yoga, working with the various forms of the divine, both externally and internally, as a means of embodying the fullness of life, and infusing one's being with a variety of powerful feminine expressions. My teacher's goal in those instructions was to have my mind, body, and emotions integrated for my actual in-the-world life.

When I started my studies in Jungian psychology, I quickly realized that my engagement with this form of Deity Yoga was quintessential archetypal work, done through a slightly different lens. The process of engaging with a female archetype as a means of invoking and assimilating her powerful positive attributes can be done within or outside of the context of spirituality or religion. It is equally powerful with any role model, pop-culture icon, or religious depiction.

My current work reflects the integration of a lifetime of study, including my first love of Celtic myth, my many years of clinical work, and my rigorous training in the feminine embodiment practices of my lineage.

....

The most important teaching I received . . . is courageous engagement with life itself, finding the divine and creating meaning in even the most simple and mundane activities.

....

The most important teaching I received, though, both through my teachers and my life experience, is courageous engagement with life itself, finding the divine and creating meaning in even the most simple and mundane activities. I strongly believe that by engaging regularly in very simple, easy-to-achieve practices, we can reconnect to our innate feminine wisdom without adding yet another "to-do" to our already full lives. As my teacher used to tell me, "The best practice is the one you actually do."

2

The Plight of the Modern Woman

I REMEMBER THE DISTINCT MOMENT WHEN I REALIZED THAT I HAD TOO many options in my life. I had just relocated to Germany and moved in with my relatively new boyfriend. It was the first time I had ever lived with a partner, and we had rented the first floor of a beautiful villa bordering the forest. It all felt very grown-up, with proper designer furniture, beautiful artwork, and a perfectly equipped kitchen. My teacher Deepa was moving to Germany, so I relocated to follow her, as I would do on several occasions in my twenties. Conveniently, my boyfriend, whom I had met while he was on a work trip to Vienna, lived in a nearby city, and I made the decision to move in with him.

I was suddenly "playing house" while I waited for my work papers. Whole days stretched out in front of me, with nothing to do except go shopping and cook an evening meal for the two of us.

As I sat looking out into the beautiful garden, I considered my many options in life: work and career, marriage and children, a spiritual life, traveling perhaps, or writing some papers; and in the short term, I had the options of reading, going for a walk, and making new friends.

As I was pondering what my life would be like, I suddenly realized that I needed to make some choices. If I married this man, who had a high-powered career, then children would be next. I imagined myself keeping the house as I did and staying home to raise, love, and care for my imaginary children the way my stay-at-home mother raised me.

But what about my ambitions? Would I still be employable after having raised my children for their formative years? Would I have to stop my studies and practices if I got pregnant now? And what if I waited a few years, invested all my time and energy building my career, and then left to raise my children?

And, even more important to me, what about my esoteric explorations? So far, studying and learning from my teachers and reading and practicing what I had learned had been the most important part of my life. How would I reconcile that path with having a boyfriend/husband? (My then boyfriend, by the way, knew next to nothing of the esoteric part of my life, and I thought he would not approve of it.)

The more I pondered this, the more despondent I became. I tried practicing yoga, dancing, meditating, reading, and engaging in the rituals I was learning at the time. I threw myself into cleaning the house and cooking elaborate meals while considering what direction my life would take.

But within a few weeks, I had gotten so depressed that I would wake up with my boyfriend, make him breakfast, and the moment he left for work, go back to bed. That's where I stayed all day, every day, in a kind of twilight space until 4:00 p.m., when I would get up, clean the kitchen, make a meal, and welcome my boyfriend home, pretending that I had had a great day.

This went on until my teacher arrived; she was appalled by my sluggish energy and obvious depressive mood. She suggested I get a volunteer job until my residency papers arrived and encouraged me to make changes to my environment, my routines, and even my appearance. I rearranged furniture, created a small private area just for myself, started the day with a walk, and in an impulsive moment of impatience, cut my long hair into a short bob (a decision that altered my appearance dramatically—and not for the better!). Slowly these (mostly) small daily changes brought me back to my usual vital self.

Gradually, I emerged from the haze of indecision and frozen boredom. I realized that I did not have to make these choices all at once and could let my life unfold.

It happened that these few months taught me more about depressive states than all my later counseling experience ever did. I had had the opinion that depression and indecision were for the chemically imbalanced and weak. In the aftermath, I came to a much better understanding of these states, which allowed me to work as a teacher and relationship counselor with greater compassion and care.

As it turns out, I had had a firsthand encounter with "The Plight of the Modern Woman." I had the privilege of more options than ever, but at the same time, I became aware that I still carried the biological imperative to bear and raise children. There were too many things I wanted to do, and I could not decide which ones I wanted. I realized then that there is simply no way to have a career, raise your own children yourself, have a spiritual life, travel, be creative, and maintain a deep intimate sexual relationship without something having to give. Not only are there only so many hours in the day, but certain requirements seem irreconcilable. Nevertheless, my youth and stubbornness made me determined that I would figure this out and have it all. Now, almost thirty years later, I can examine this time with hindsight.

As women in the "first world," we do have many more options than our grandmothers had. By no means are we "there" yet, but looking back at history, we have more choice, freedom, and opportunity than ever before. We also experience significantly more stress, as the pace of life has rapidly increased and the sheer volume of inflow, information, stimulation, and demand has outpaced our bodies and brains.

In addition, we as women must still consider our biological clocks. However, we are among the first few generations who can choose when we want to get pregnant. More than anything else, the Pill, which became available in 1960, has liberated women and given us opportunity and freedom.

Not only were some of our mothers and even some of our grandmothers free to have the sex they wanted, with whom they wanted, without having to fear unwanted pregnancy, most importantly, they could suddenly make choices about their careers and lives as well.

Starting in 2009, for the first time in US history, women have overtaken men in professional roles. Now women represent half of all US workers and are the primary or co-breadwinners in nearly two-thirds of American households.

This is partly because the current economy requires that both men and women earn an income, and partly because women can now make the choice as to when to have children and can plan their careers, lives, and circumstances accordingly.

Gloria Feldt, the former CEO and president of Planned Parenthood and author of *No Excuses: 9 Ways Women Can Change How We Think about Power*, now in her mid-seventies, says, "As someone who had three children by the time she was 20, the pill literally saved my life. Without the pill, I would have had one or two more. It enabled me to purposefully have a life that I designed. It allowed me to start college and begin a career."[2]

Feldt says, "If women are going to have control and power in society, they have to be able to control when they have children, and they have to be able to make money. The pill brought together the economics and the fertility timeline in a neat little package."[3]

We are now privileged to have a choice as to if, and when, we have children. Birth control gives us freedom and power. (Defunding of birth control options for low-income women takes away their choice and freedom more than anything else does.)

However, even with choice, our fertility, youth, energy, and capacity are all intricately tied to our bodies. The years that are most fertile for developing a career are also our most reproductively fertile years.

Theoretically, we can have it all—the neat package of career and family—but on a practical level, the demands on our bodies alone make it such that, at some point, choices must be made. We suffer physically through the way energy moves in our bodies when we work. The focus on mental activity and engagement with electronic devices, combined with sitting still for long periods of time, brings our energy upward toward the head. We suffer from tight neck, shoulders, and jaw, tension headaches and mental overload. High-stress activity weakens and dis-embodies us by using up available physical resources, and we lose both softness and creativity.

Being in the world requires that we animate our internal mascu-line, the part of us that kicks ass and takes names later. Our creative, relational feminine side often becomes relegated to the off hours and therefore begins to wither.

....

> Being in the world requires that we animate our internal masculine, the part of us that kicks ass and takes names later. Our creative, relational feminine side often becomes relegated to the off hours and therefore begins to wither.

....

We see many wonderful, accomplished, and kind women not being able to find lasting relationships or suffering from imbalances in their existing relationships. Often, I encounter women who no longer have a choice between career and family because they haven't been able to get beyond the first few dates with a man.

We'll go into details of the various aspects of relationship in a later chapter, but one of the main challenges lies in the simple fact that work life and romantic life require diametrically opposite dispositions.

When every day, all day, is filled with doing, coping, and striving, we take on the corresponding "psycho-emotional asana" in our nervous system. I call it an "asana," a term used in yoga to denote posture, because as in yoga, the repetition of the posture is what creates habit. As in yoga, we can change in and out of postures at will, if we know what our options are.

Whatever we do most in our day-to-day lives forms the shape of our habits, physically, emotionally, and mentally. Daily push to get things done, focus, and direction all create a shape—a habit-pattern of posture, emotional content, and external behavior that gets stronger with the "practice" of doing it every day.

....

Whatever we do most in our day-to-day lives forms the shape of our habits, physically, emotionally, and mentally. Daily push to get things done, focus, and direction all create a shape—a habit-pattern of posture, emotional content, and external behavior that gets stronger with the "practice" of doing it every day.

....

The "asana" of perpetual doing, coping, and striving is an unnatural position for a woman desiring an intimate partner. The feminine shape for interacting with a partner is a softening, receiving, and opening disposition—the opposite of the "push" of doing. We sometimes spontaneously see this softening, receiving part of ourselves when we fall in love. People comment on how radiant and happy we look. But if we are in the habit of assuming a "pushing" disposition most hours of the day, that becomes our default expression.

When it comes time to engage with our partners—or potential

partners—our "energetic romance muscles" are not sufficiently trained, and we are not able to shift easily into the mode that allows for romance, connection, intimacy, and pleasure.

In this scenario, one of two things happens. We either repel the partners we want, or we "depolarize" the partners we have. To explain what I mean by "depolarize": In an intimate relationship, there are always two poles. We can call them "masculine/feminine" or "go/flow." It is not necessarily gender-specific, but both need to be present for a connection to have sexual attraction and chemistry. When one partner animates one aspect, the other assumes the other. When both are in "flow" or both are in "go," the relationship becomes sexually depolarized and the partners lose attraction. (We'll cover this some more in chapter 13, "Relationships," pp. 159–171.)

Understanding the dynamics of attraction, along with training the body to be able to assume "go" as well as "flow" modes fluidly, allows us to realistically have both a career and a relationship. This requires practicing whatever mode we are not accustomed to practicing, which for many of us is the feminine.

> Understanding the dynamics of attraction, along with training the body to be able to assume "go" as well as "flow" modes fluidly, allows us to realistically have both a career and a relationship.

When we are able to move fluidly and consciously between the two modes, we can be effective in our careers and daily life, and enjoy the erotic tension of relationship. Though we still need to make decisions around time and energy, we are no longer held back by lack of facility in switching between modes.

But relationship and career are not the only two choices for a fulfilling life. Within the relationship, or in the face of not having one, we

need to decide not only when but also *if* we want children. There is also
the engagement with ourselves, taking care of our health, our bodies,
and our souls. We might also want to engage in further education, in
the realm of self-development or learning new professional skills. And
finally, we need time for leisure, travel, and fun.

One could say that having this much choice is a quality problem, and
that there are many women who are not so fortunate. As much as this is
true, it nevertheless is a serious consideration. Unless we want to stumble
from one relationship to the next and one job to another, we will need to
make decisions about where best to spend our time and energy.

So how do we make choices? And how do we know these are the
best choices for us? As with most women's issues, opinions and information diverge greatly on this. On one hand, the message is that we
should not squander the opportunities our mothers and grandmothers
fought so hard for, that we should "lean in" and claim positions of
power and forge a strong career path. On the other hand, there is the
not-so-subtle-anymore promise of a glorious domestic life, expressed
in various ways: the DIY fantasies of Pinterest; the simple living
movement; the green-urban-farmstead-backyard-chicken-hipster life
and the numerous chic lifestyle brands and websites enticing us to
make beautiful, nutritious meals, buy products and participate in
treatments for a radiantly healthy body, and create a beautifully decorated home.

The strong influence of social media adds more grist to the mill
of potential decision-making. We compare our lives to the Instagram
and Facebook posts showing other people having perfect bodies, perfect
homes, adventurous trips to exotic locations, and living perfect, happy
lives. We have become used to carefully curated and hence totally unrealistic depictions of what our lives could look like.

I call this "lifestyle porn," and it is as dangerous and detrimental as
the real thing. The aspirational depiction of what life supposedly should
look like is as harmful to women's development as actual porn is to

men's. It creates unrealistic expectations, programs a fantasy view of life, and numbs us to the real thing. At best, it might provide inspiration and perhaps a competitive motivation; at worst, it leaves us with a feeling of constant lack and insecurity.

....

We have become used to carefully curated and hence totally
unrealistic depictions of what our life could look like.
I call this "lifestyle porn," and it is as dangerous
and detrimental as the real thing.

....

There is an upside to all of this, however. We do live in a time and age in which we no longer need to conform nearly as much as previous generations did. We are exposed to more information, education, and opportunities. We can work from home, pursue entrepreneurial enterprises, or even create our own YouTube channels and become internet sensations. We can have intimate relationships that are less traditional and create our lives in many "alternative" ways.

If you know who you are, these options can help you tremendously. Knowing what you are about and what you want from your life is the first step in making empowered choices. And this is where the Wild Woman comes in.

The Wild Woman is about connecting to your instinctive nature, your true expression. It means tuning in to your body's rhythms, listening to your instincts, and honing your own unique way of moving through the world, while availing yourself of the age-old wisdom that lies within the collective feminine consciousness. It takes courage to uncover this wildness and to see through the conditioning and programming of modern life, but when you are able to listen to the signals of your body and include your intuition and your conscious mind in the decision-making process, all aspects of your being become involved, and previously hidden caches of wisdom and guidance emerge from within.

You are no longer choosing based on convention or societal requirements, or only from your head; instead, you are making empowered decisions using your whole system—body, mind, and spirit—in an intelligent and embodied way.

3

Women and the Feminine

LARA WAS ONE OF THE MANY WOMEN WHO CAME TO ME IN A QUEST to become more feminine. She told us that, as a single mother, she had started dating recently and had two unsuccessful relationships. Both times the men had broken up with her, citing that she was "not feminine enough."

After the first breakup, she had started taking pole dancing classes and invested in some sexy lingerie to become what she thought would be "more feminine." During her most recent relationship, she had tried being more seductive in the way she had learned in pole class, and had attempted to connect more physically, through touching and hugging. Despite her best attempts, this relationship had lasted barely six months.

After Lara answered a few questions about her behavior and what the men had actually said to her, we came to the bottom of the issue, which was a lot more multilayered than simply her lack of feminine wiles.

Lara was a single mother of a five-year-old boy. Both men had picked up on a tendency Lara had developed while raising her little boy by herself. She often treated her boyfriends with the same kind of strong, motherly direction she gave her son. She had gotten into the habit of being in charge and taking control, which is perfectly appropriate for raising a child, but not so much when relating to a grown man.

Once she came to understand this pattern, she could also see, as others did, that her attention toward the men was very motherly. She laughed and cringed as she told us that her idea of being intimate often included patting her partners' heads when they were tired and offering them food and cookies. Comforting, yes; sexy—not so much!

Having realized these behaviors, she was able to see how she needed to bring the woman she was, and not the mother, to the sexual aspects of her relationship. There are appropriate times for nurturing, as well as times for strongly making one's needs known, in every relationship. For the erotic aspect of the relationship, pleasure in the body and an ability to express that pleasure with a partner, are what create excitement and chemistry. (We'll cover more of this in chapter 9, "Pleasure Is Our Birthright" pp. 113–129, and chapter 13, "Relationships" pp. 159–171.)

....

For the erotic aspect of the relationship, pleasure in the body and an ability to express that pleasure with a partner, are what create excitement and chemistry.

....

The insidious aspect of Lara's story is her assumption about what makes her "more feminine." Upon closer examination, it turned out that she had bought into some classic stereotypes. She had tried emulating other women's expressions instead of finding her own. Much like a high school student, she had oriented herself to what the "cool, sexy girls" were doing and tried her best to emulate their behavior.

In pole dancing class, she had tried her hand at "sexy stripper" and attempted to play that role when her boyfriend came home. When she went to a women's yoga class, she tried her best to emulate the "California goddess vibe" of the teacher and dressed in sparkling, multicolored garb. With everything she tried, she put on (what she thought was) the feminine expression as if she were putting on a costume. None of it was felt in her body, and her tension around getting it right made her even less connected.

She felt that she was performing an act and disconnected from herself, her body, and any feelings of sensual pleasure. To make matters worse, the men she dated and the courses she took made her feel that her job as an accountant was to blame for her lack of femininity. She told us she had considered changing her profession, since she so desperately wanted a relationship.

Lara's story is all too common. Some variation of this narrative shows up in every single workshop I give, and many women who come from this disconnected perspective express great confusion and frustration about trying to navigate dating, relationship, and sex.

"Being in our feminine" has become quite the buzzword and the prescription for all that ails us as women. But what does this actually mean?

The term "feminine" can be very confusing, often conflating "woman" and "feminine," and often also implying that in order to be feminine, certain criteria must be fulfilled. On the West Coast of the US, where I live, it often means certain flowy, boho-chic clothing, Burning-Man-esque getups, and sparkling adornments. In other parts of the world, I have encountered goddess circles, striptease classes, and detailed instructions on how to make sexy sounds, among other offerings.

In reality, the terms "masculine" and "feminine" mean different things to different people. Feminism and gender studies see the term "feminine" in a descriptive way, and the dictionary describes it as "having qualities or appearance traditionally associated with women, especially delicacy and prettiness." Hence the strong association between "women" and "feminine."

The most popular use of the term these days comes from Tantric teachings and their offshoots. In the Tantric system, each human being has two aspects, referred to as "Shiva" and "Shakti"—the divine expressions present in each human.

Shiva, the masculine aspect, is the part of each of us that gets things done. Shiva is the principle of linear doing, striving, planning, and grid-like focus, the part of us that organizes and creates order out of chaos.

Shakti, the feminine aspect, is the undulating, pulsating force that is nature itself, the part of us that is creative chaos.

One of these aspects without the other is useless. Both need to be present at all times for any human being to function. In both men and women, these two aspects are equally present. Where it becomes interesting is when we look at partnership, either within ourselves, as in integrating and balancing those two aspects, or in romantic relationship.

The Tantric teachings around attraction center on one partner animating one aspect strongly, while the other partner goes to the opposite aspect. This makes for two distinct poles. The stronger the poles are, the stronger the sexual attraction. When I teach people how to make themselves "different poles" for the sake of that attraction, it sometimes feels like magic. When the simple principle of "making yourself different" is applied, it can create an immediate strong spark. This is the sort of spark that lovers feel on first meeting, those electric first months of the honeymoon period which is so often lost as time goes by. Contrary to popular belief, this isn't just the domain of fate, chance, and magic, but something that can be consciously created and nurtured with the right understanding and practice.

Within this viewpoint, the term "feminine" refers to being able to assume a certain "psycho-emotional asana," which has a bodily, emotional, and mental component. Since the demands of everyday life are mostly centered around the masculine expression, most women are no longer skilled in animating their feminine. We have trained ourselves to be directed, assertive, tough, and efficient, attributes which correspond with bodily skills that are very valuable but not useful when we want to relax, surrender, feel, and flow. It is the equivalent of not having played the piano in twenty years and going onstage to play a concert. You might remember some of what you learned long before, but actual physical practice is what created your ability to play well, and also what brings it back. Relaxing the body; engaging with life, beauty, and nature; and gentle, nonlinear movement and dance are some of those physical practices we'll be engaging in throughout this book.

Men have a feminine too, and it also needs to be practiced and cultivated for sensitivity, feeling, creativity, and expression. Ideally, each human being has both masculine and feminine aspects well developed in his or her body so s/he can use both whenever s/he needs and wants to.

Developing feminine skills does not mean being a bimbo or a stripper or becoming a pushover. It just means that in moments where sexual chemistry is desired, whoever enjoys playing the feminine is able to assume that receptive and soft posture.

....

> Developing feminine skills does not mean being a bimbo or a stripper or becoming a pushover. It just means that in moments where sexual chemistry is desired, whoever enjoys playing the feminine is able to assume that receptive and soft posture.

....

This brings us to the topic of preference. Most of us have a sexual-relational preference, meaning a native inclination in which we feel happiest and most expressed. For many women that is their feminine, which is conveyed through a creative, colorful fullness, a moving, undulating disposition that feels and expresses through emotions and the body. That preference expressed unfolds through communion, collaboration, beauty, adornments, music, food, and abundance.

Yet that preference looks very different from woman to woman, and finding one's authentic expression is more important than fitting in with the prevailing zeitgeist or the prescribed sexy activity of the month.

Some women express very opulently, and others have an almost Zen-like starkness in their internal and external expression.

Then there are women who truly prefer resting in what is considered the masculine, which is just as fine, as long as they are aware of the laws of erotic tension. There has to be one of each pole in the relationship to create the spark, which would mean that they are best matched with a man who prefers to live out the receiving disposition sexually. This does not mean that the man is in any way effeminate, it simply means that in this case, the woman is the driving force and the man is the creative swirl when it comes to the erotic.

If your sexual style tends toward surrender and letting go, your preference, sexually speaking, is the feminine pole. If your preferred sexual expression is dominant, taking, and penetrating, then you would be considered as having a masculine preference. Of course, most people like to play in both, which is why having full range of expression is so important.

. . . .

> If your sexual style tends toward surrender and letting go, your
> preference, sexually speaking, is the feminine pole. If your preferred
> sexual expression is dominant, taking, and penetrating, then
> you would be considered as having a masculine preference.

. . . .

This concept is extremely useful when it comes to figuring out how to switch between career mode and romantic mode, but it is simply a tool and not a heal-all or a lifestyle recommendation.

The most important thing to remember in reconnecting with our feminine is that one expression does not fit all. When, as in Lara's case, the expression is not truly born from the sensual awareness of one's own body, alive and animated through one's deepest heart, it becomes a shallow facsimile of the real thing. The sacredness of the feminine comes from a true, heartfelt, embodied wisdom being expressed in the unique shape of each woman and not from wearing the right kind of lingerie or feather boa.

Putting on a persona of someone else's expression, or trying to emulate the current gold standard of social media femininity, is just adopting a fake layer in order to be someone we are not. In many ways, it is the revival of the fifties-housewife scenario with a neo-Tantric twist.

> Putting on a persona of someone else's expression, or trying to emulate the current gold standard of social media femininity, is just adopting a fake layer in order to be someone we are not. In many ways, it is the revival of the fifties-housewife scenario with a neo-Tantric twist.

I sometimes refer to this as the "New Domestication of Women," which, through its conflation of "masculine" with men and "feminine" with women, reinforces traditional gender roles, just in a slightly modernized way.

The "feminine" in this scenario becomes just another box to be put in, a slightly more spiritual approach that renders men into supermasculine warriors in response to their cookie-cutter, sacred-feminine-pleasure goddesses.

That view creates an extremely disempowering scenario. In it, men are the strong, unmoving space holders, and women turn into damsels in distress or raging furies, a far cry from what happens in actual life. Playing with polarity in the bedroom is extremely useful for keeping the spark alive, but as a model for living, it does not do the current cultural realities justice. It reduces our vast human potential to gender roles that are entirely outdated, if they have ever actually been true.

The fact is, many women enjoy their careers, their professional competence, and their independence. They would not want to give those up just so they can be considered feminine. Many men nowadays have developed their sensitivity, and even the most rugged, silent types have learned that they can—and want to—connect with and express their feelings on occasion.

The dogmatic approach to the terms "masculine" and "feminine" being interchangeable with "men" and "women" begets confusion, and reduces our vast potential as humans.

In order for our inner masculine and feminine to be integrated and put to good use, we must accept, cultivate, and revere both aspects. The same is true in the dance of the genders—and it can be a dance, not a war. By accepting, cultivating, and revering both men and women for their unique gifts, we accept and honor their differences. For true healing and integration to occur, we must see a much bigger context: sacred human beings, each with a heart, a mind, emotions, and a spiritual purpose, all of it precious, distinct, and worthwhile.

....

> In order for our inner masculine and feminine to be
> integrated and put to good use, we must accept,
> cultivate, and revere both aspects.

....

From the place of accepting both aspects within ourselves, we can cultivate the aspect our heart desires most to express, which for many women is the feminine. By honoring our masculine capacities, we can cultivate them further and put them to excellent use.

We can choose freely from a vast variety of expression and tools, and approach each moment, each situation, fresh, using the aspect that is most applicable and beneficial at the time, instead of being driven by unexamined knee-jerk reactions and habitual responses.

As for Lara, she began to explore what her true, natural feminine expression was and made it a daily practice to spend some time in that disposition. She began each day by dancing to one song, to engage with her body before going to work. She found a simple way to stay focused and organized in her work, without adding extra tension, by taking a five-minute break from sitting each hour to stretch, drink water, and relax tension patterns in her body. She adopted a few simple ways to switch out of accountant mode before she came home to her son—singing loudly in the car, or sitting on a bench close to her house and being with nature before she went home. On the evenings she is going out for a date, she dances around the house beforehand, to get into her body, and most evenings she enjoys a bath before bedtime.

Over time, she has been able to claim her sensuality and express it with the man she is now dating by allowing him to see her joy and pleasure in the body. She no longer tries to "do" sexy—she simply *is* sexy in her very own way.

She reports that the engagement with her sensual body has had another interesting side effect. She was suddenly able to set better boundaries with her son's father, and their relationship and communication has improved. She now also feels proud of her ability with numbers and accounting, instead of seeing it as a hindrance to her romantic life.

Engaging with our very own feminine expression and cultivating our unique gifts are sacred. We become an offering to those we meet, and can connect through our bodies, our intuition, and our wisdom. And most importantly, we can do so without leaving any part of ourselves behind.

....

> Engaging with our very own feminine expression
> and cultivating our unique gifts are sacred.

....

Here is a simple way to reconnect with flow and become aware of the sensations in your body: Take a moment to notice your body. Have you been sitting still while reading this? Are you relaxed and comfort-

able or is there tension anywhere? Start by feeling your body in the chair
and begin moving subtly. Wiggle your toes and stretch your feet. Bring
a bit of undulation into your spine and move with whatever you are
feeling. Focus primarily on areas that feel good, expanding the pleasant
sensations through your movements. Allow yourself to take this moment to just be with the sensations in your body.

4

Re-wilding the Feminine

FOR MONTHS, I HAD IMAGINED THIS MOMENT. I WOULD VISUALIZE myself sitting on the ground, looking up into a big oak tree, and know that this was my home. This little piece of earth was mine to decorate, restore, and steward. Every time I envisioned receiving the keys to my own first house, my eyes would brim with tears of joy and longing. It felt so right, even though I still wasn't sure it was really going to happen.

Through a series of events that were nothing short of miraculous, I was now in escrow for the property of my dreams. I had always wanted to own a house, but living in an area of Los Angeles where a shack sold for about a million dollars and having been self-employed for most of my career made that dream seem unattainable.

For the past fifteen years, I had lived in an incredibly busy and densely populated area of West Hollywood, with sirens, helicopters, ambulances, and constant traffic noise. My office overlooked a major intersection, and every corner of the city was being built up with malls, cinemas, and high-end condos.

I had become used to the constant noise, and even though I was intellectually aware of the numbing effect of the constant stimuli, I was no longer aware of how it affected my nervous system. My days were packed with clients, driving, computer work, and travel.

Then one day we received a notice that the small, flat mall right across from our street was being demolished, and a twelve-story multi-use building with stores and condos would take its place. The thought of three years of constant construction noise, traffic, and dust less than five hundred yards from my bedroom was more than I could handle. In that instant I made the decision to leave Los Angeles.

The practicalities of such a move were difficult; I could see clients only in my office in LA, and back then, Skype sessions were not widely offered. Nevertheless, over the next six months, circumstances conspired in such a way that I found myself in escrow on several acres of land, a ninety-minute drive from my office and far enough outside the little town of Ojai, California, to feel like rural countryside.

It came with old oak growth, a stone house, and access to the national forest and swimming holes right behind my fence. The property had never left the family who had homesteaded it, and the sellers were in their eighties and had lived there all their lives. It was everything I had ever wished for: privacy, room for farm animals, a vegetable patch, thirty varieties of fruit trees and avocados, large rocks emerging from the ground, and a workshop space that I could convert to a studio to practice and teach in.

There had been a lot of complications, everything from having to put down a very large deposit, to zoning issues, to a previously interested buyer making trouble, to the sudden crash in the housing market and the disappearance of the kind of loan I needed as a self-employed woman. I had been on an intense three-month roller coaster and did not know until the day escrow closed whether it would all come together. But it did, and there we were, taking possession of the keys.

I can still feel the weak-in-the-knees elation I felt driving onto the property. Much to our surprise, there was a man on a tractor mowing the front field! Turns out it was the day of the fire department's brush clearance deadline and our next-door neighbor figured he could take care of it for us quickly!

Within the few minutes it took us to park and get out of the car, several people had appeared. Someone handed my husband a beer and me a glass of champagne. Our new neighbors all showed up to welcome us, the Realtor drove the old couple who were the sellers up from their assisted living facility to meet us, and within an hour we had a lively party going on our new patio.

Everyone talked and drank, and more neighbors arrived with food. The previous owner took me through the orchards, where she had affixed a little metal tag to each tree with the name of the tree variety written on it, and told me when and how she had planted this or that tree and what the fruit tasted like.

The former man of the house took my husband aside and, with twinkling eyes, instructed him on how to effectively aim to shoot a gopher, which shocked and amused my inner animal-loving, city-girl self.

Embraced so fully by our neighbors, we suddenly found ourselves in a functioning community—not one that was meant as a social experiment to live sustainably or intentionally, but one based on real relationships among people living with neighbors in a somewhat remote area. Since it takes twenty minutes to get to the next gas station or store, everyone helps one another. We trade eggs for help with a broken faucet, share resources, support each other through emergencies, and get together for meals and celebrations.

We are an odd mix of people: some come from families who homesteaded the area; some are artists, writers, acupuncturists; some are retired; and we even have a resident psychic! About half of our little community are of other nationalities and there are about as many liberals as there are conservatives. It was a real adjustment from having lived in the anonymity of large cities my whole adult life.

Over the next year, I settled into the routine of commuting to my office three days a week and spending the rest of my time renovating the house and planting and cultivating the land. I rescued my first goat, whom I found tied to the side of the road with a "For Sale— Good Meat" sign next to her. I purchased her for twenty dollars and loaded her into the back of my car, much to the amusement of the men selling her.

Gradually, my nervous system reset itself. I did not notice at first, busy as I was with commuting, renovation, and settling in. But soon it became apparent that my body had started to unwind. Sleeping in absolute silence, with no light at night, no air pollution, and fresh water straight out of my well, I became more aware of my body, more sensitized to myself and the people I interacted with. My body benefitted from all the gardening, walking, and hiking, and my sleep improved. My intuition came back online and my creativity soared.

I noticed that I was no longer attached to my phone or computer. My friends would complain that I would not return their texts or e-mails for the whole day, which was unheard of. My priorities had shifted. I still worked as hard as I ever had, but the work was interspersed with periods of simple gardening and caring for my ever-increasing number of rescue animals.

I discovered that being part of a community has incredible benefits. The knowledge that there was help and support around me was tremendously calming in a way I had never anticipated. When a water pipe breaks and the driveway is showered by a geyser, a quick call to Rod, my neighbor who can fix absolutely anything, will remedy it. When I feel social, I lean over a fence for a chat or pop by a neighbor's house for a drink; but if I need privacy, everyone is incredibly respectful. I truly feel part of a "tribe," which was surprising and such a gift.

Over the years, I built a teaching studio on the property and eventually gave up my office in Los Angeles. Now I work while looking over the pasture where the donkeys play, and even though I travel for large parts of the year, this is truly my home. It has become the inspiration for much of my creative output and provides a solid home base for my life. Looking back, I can say that my land has truly re-wilded me.

So, what is re-wilding? The dictionary describes it as "restoring [something] to its natural uncultivated state." It is a return to our original nature. This does not mean that you have to move to the countryside and grow your own vegetables! Re-wilding looks different for each woman; the key is to find what opens your heart and relaxes your body, and, with that, allows you to be unabashedly you.

> Re-wilding looks different for each woman; the key is
> to find what opens your heart and relaxes your body,
> and, with that, allows you to be unabashedly you.

When we re-wild ourselves, we are stripping away layers of behavior, persona, and coping, and feeling who we really are underneath. We return to feeling through the body and trusting in what is felt. The emphasis is on relaxation and release, instead of on pushing and "improving" oneself in order to be "good enough."

Re-wilding means connecting with and celebrating what has always been there—our instinctual, natural abilities—which are the core of who we are. From there we can expand outward, developing skills that allow for our full potential to be expressed freely.

There are four major aspects to re-wilding: embodiment, sensitization, relaxation, and release. You will find detailed practical exercises for all these aspects in section IV: "Sacred Practices of the Wild Woman," pp. 197–236.

Embodiment is one of the major aspects of my work. We'll go into much more detail in chapter 6: "Embodiment," pp. 71–81. What makes embodiment such an important component is that innate wisdom lies in the body, and only by being in and feeling the body do we have access to our full potential. Re-wilding uncovers the natural genius of the body.

> ....
>
> Re-wilding uncovers the natural genius of the body.
>
> ....

Sensitization allows each of us to perceive more of what our body, a finely tuned instrument, is telling us. We gain access to feeling. This includes pleasure and, of course, all other emotions. When we sensitize, we naturally begin to feel how to regulate ourselves in eating, exercising, and relating to others.

Relaxation aids in embodiment and sensitization. It frees energy held in the unnecessary tension in the body. Relaxation also allows the body to restore and repair. There are many ways to relax: sleeping, engaging in less "doing," taking time to meditate, and giving actual attention to relaxing the muscles to rid them of unnecessary tension.

A major aspect of re-wilding is letting go of unnecessary "push" and tension. Most of us, because of the way we are trained, add a lot of extra effort to what we are doing. Doing, in itself, implies effort, and it's true that we do need to contract muscles to move; but which muscles do we truly need to engage, and how much of the tension is extra?

The extra tension is a coping mechanism. We clench physically because of stress and strain. We brace against emotional overwhelm. We enter into thought loops in the hope of figuring things out. You might feel your face pinch, your pelvic floor tighten, and your voice constrict. This extra tension can be relaxed, which frees a lot of energy for the actual activity at hand. It is a bit counterintuitive, but once you get the concept, you can feel the benefits immediately.

When working on relaxation, I often call attention to the "push." The solar plexus is the central area of the push. Strain and stress contract and harden the area of the solar plexus and the diaphragm. When the diaphragm is contracted, our breathing becomes shallow and high in the chest, depriving us of oxygen, and the fight-or-flight impulse gets activated in the nervous system, setting in an even stronger stress response.

The solar plexus is an area of strong feeling. It is sometimes called the "second brain." Many traditions see it as the seat of intuition and wisdom. People will talk about a "gut feeling" and point to their solar plexus. If you experience chronic tension and push, the area becomes numb and hard, and you lose access to those feelings.

....

The solar plexus is an area of strong feeling. It is sometimes called the "second brain." Many traditions see it as the seat of intuition and wisdom.

....

Exercise for Solar Plexus Relaxation

Take a moment and sit in an upright but comfortable posture. Put your hand on the area halfway between your sternum and your belly button and, for a moment, use your fingers to gently press in. Notice if the area is tight and resists the pressing. Do you feel any emotion, irritation, or tightness there?

In the Tantric tradition this area is associated with our expression in the world and with personal power. Physically, we experience tightness in the solar plexus when we have to work hard to assert ourselves.

Locate a spot in that area that draws you and rest your hand on it. Notice the sensations that arise from the touch. Can you feel the warmth of your hand? Is the feeling pleasant, neutral, or unpleasant? Now begin breathing in a way that creates a visible movement of your hand. See if you can expand the area on the inhale and relax it under your hand with each exhale. You can experiment with the length and depth of each breath and rub the area in an upward, circular motion.

You might not feel anything to begin with, or maybe you experience a volcano of emotion and feeling. Neither is better than the other; simply becoming familiar with that part of your body will support relaxation over time, and with that, increased awareness of the signals of your "second brain."

Release is the final aspect of re-wilding. It allows our body to let go of past trauma, heartache, and disappointment. As much as we might have dealt with these things in our minds by speaking about them with friends and therapists, and in workshops, the body does not forget them.

When emotions get suppressed or held in our bodies, we develop patterns of contraction and protection. These patterns get activated when similar emotions arise again, or the activities that first caused the contractions are being performed. The contraction activates, and keeps us from feeling the entirety of the emotion.

....

> When emotions get suppressed or held in our bodies, we develop patterns of contraction and protection. These patterns get activated when similar emotions arise again, or the activities that first caused the contractions are being performed.

....

For instance, I have an "extreme workload" coping pattern that manifests in rolling forward my right shoulder, as if I were pushing against something heavy. I became aware of the pattern only when my shoulder developed chronic pain. In tracing the pattern, I realized that it was connected from my forehead all the way to my thighs via a subtle but persistent clench. When I started releasing the clench through specific movement—which I will introduce you to in detail later—the emotions connected with the clench started to surface.

I came in touch with a feeling of being left alone, overwhelmed, and helpless; the tension pattern was an attempt to cover those feelings by "sucking it up and getting to work." Now, whenever I feel the pattern appearing, I can relax the contraction and notice the emotional story of "coping alone without help," release the story, and instead deal with the reality in front of me.

This is possible only because I have become sensitized to my body and can feel the very beginning of this insidious and unhealthy pattern. Needless to say, I am not always successful in catching it, but whenever I do, I can release it, which brings me to the present moment and frees the contracted energy to be used for what really needs attention.

By tracing our physical patterns, we can become aware of our "stories" of old pain, hurts, and happenings that still influence us. We might not even be aware of how much our actions are influenced by those bygone emotions and events. Or we are aware yet don't know how to let them go, as they are inextricably connected with our somatic patterns. Instead of using emotion to work with the body, you can let the body show you where and how it stores or covers up emotion. That way you get to release both the physical patterns and the pent-up emotions. You will learn how to do this effectively through The Non-Linear Movement Method®, described in section IV: "Sacred Practices of the Wild Woman," pp. 197–236.

> By tracing our physical patterns, we can become aware of our "stories" of old pain, hurts, and happenings that still influence us. We might not even be aware of how much our actions are influenced by those bygone emotions and events.

As you start to re-wild, you'll become aware of old emotional patterns via contractions of the body. You'll free energy which can be used to express who you are now instead of repeating an old story stuck in your body from days gone by. By feeling more and more accurately, you can become more effective with your energy and your boundaries and enjoy the pleasure that is always already in your body.

....

By feeling more and more accurately, you can become
more effective with your energy and your boundaries and
enjoy the pleasure that is always already in your body.

....

How then did my little farm in Ojai re-wild me? After many years of building a career as a teacher; counseling for more than forty thousand hours; traveling as a consultant and bearing the heavy workload and the resulting stress, the sensory overload of living in such an intense place as Los Angeles, and the lack of community there, I was brought back to my original nature. Once I relocated and engaged with my land, started growing herbs and vegetables, rescued and cared for animals, and had meaningful human interactions, my body, mind, and soul opened and relaxed.

Through my body, I could connect to what was dearest to my heart, and the simple activities of gardening and caring for my animals released old stored emotion and tension from within. The absence of noise and light pollution naturally sensitized and relaxed me, and my new community gave me a sense of belonging and safety, which did wonders for my nervous system.

My little farm in Ojai re-wilded me. Each woman has a place like this, where body, heart, and mind can remember their true nature. Your "place" might be a garden, or a ritual, or playing an instrument; you might find it by reading a book or listening to music through headphones. It could be a beach, a mountaintop, or the chair on your high-rise balcony. Pay attention to where you feel the happiest and most alive. When *you* find *your* place, your body will remember, and with the additional support of the exercises presented here, the Wild Woman you are can blossom, emerge, and express in all her glory.

If you have a desire to connect with actual earth but don't have time or access to a garden, here is a beautiful and simple practice for you:

Practice to Connect with Earth

Buy a small flowerpot and saucer and some good quality potting soil. Choose a pack of bean seeds, either from your local garden center or an on-line source. Plant a few beans and get them to sprout, grow, and eventually harvest the beans for a meal. You can grow beans inside an apartment or outside on a balcony as long as you have a window with some sun.

A bean plant may not seem like much, but encouraging the flourishing of a plant in your own space connects you powerfully to the earth and the rhythms of life. And learning to listen to the needs of the plants, as any gardener knows, is a process that is only partly analytical and very much more instinctive. I've given this assignment to many women over the years, and their engagement with their bean plant often mirrors their engagement with life itself. You'll be surprised how much discovery lies in a simple bean plant! For more in-depth instruction go to p. 230, "Gardening—Getting Your Hand in the Dirt," found in section IV: "Sacred Practices of the Wild Woman."

II

A Woman's Feeling Body

5

Energetics in a Woman's Body

CAITLIN WAS A SINGLE MOTHER, RECENTLY DIVORCED AFTER A TWELVE-year marriage. A successful lawyer who had made partner in her firm, she had spent most of her twenties and thirties working an incredible volume of hours. She explained to me that, as partner, she was obligated to bill her clients a certain number of hours per week, and that the pressure of doing so had consumed her life.

When she became a mother to her now four-year-old daughter, she wanted to spend every free moment with her child, which in turn ended the already precarious relationship she had with her husband.

Now, suddenly, she had every other weekend to herself as her daughter spent time with her father, and she decided to take better care of herself. At thirty-eight, she found herself single, overweight, and out of shape from many years of excessive sitting—and she was perpetually stressed.

Her dentist had recently discovered that Caitlin was grinding her teeth at night and had given her a stern warning to find ways to relax. Her doctor was concerned with her weight, and she had recently started to experience unpleasant hormonal imbalances, which only added more discomfort to her ongoing headaches and back pain.

As she was first introduced to the Wild Woman's Way practices, Caitlin realized that she was cut off from her body, and numb to most feelings, including the pain of her divorce and the every-other-weekend separation from her daughter. Once she started moving her body, she became acutely aware of her extra weight, the pain in her joints, and the overwhelming grief she had kept at bay by numbing herself with working and eating.

She confessed that she had planned to leave the workshop after the first day, but that during the evening's exercises, which included non-linear body movement and dance, she had a brief glimpse into something she had forgotten: how much she had loved dancing and music before she went to law school.

For that moment at the workshop, she was immersed in the rhythm, the sound, and a feeling of freedom. She had forgotten about her weight, her self-consciousness around the other women, and the sadness she felt. Underneath all of it there was an energetic, wild, and adventurous woman who just wanted to stomp her feet.

When she left that weekend, she started to dance again—just for one song a day, and often she would be so out of breath she could not even finish. She persevered through her shame of having let herself get so out of shape and kept going, driven by that feeling of freedom she had felt.

Over the course of a few weeks she noticed small changes taking place. She became aware of her posture at work and started sitting differently. She observed patterns of overeating during times of stress. And to her, most importantly, she began to feel the emotions connected to her divorce.

She joined my ongoing women's group, where she learned movement practices and other ways to connect back to herself. She danced to learn how to connect to her body and listen to its signals. She sensitized through gentle yoga and stillness to explore ways to relax her body and formed a strong connection with some of the other women in the group. She courageously began to speak about her experiences and she made movement and her body a priority.

To begin with, she would go on walks with her daughter and spend consistent time dancing each day. This led to different food choices and, at some point, she felt good enough to attend 5Rhythms® [4] classes and went hiking into the hills of her neighborhood.

Over time, she learned to better cope with everyday stresses, and finally, she decided to leave her law firm for a less demanding position as a consultant for an international charitable organization.

She now marvels at how one small change—dancing to one song a day—completely changed her life. She recalls that there weren't huge cathartic changes, but a steady awakening to feeling her body, her needs, and what was right for her.

She continues to move every day to release stress, to feel, and to connect with herself. She also dances with her daughter as often as she can, and now that she has a lot more time to spend with her, they enjoy hiking together. Recently she started dating a man who adores her and, much to her surprise, she has discovered that she has a talent for painting.

Caitlin's story of losing touch with herself and her relationships is all too common. Many women I work with experience the gradual loss of connection to the feelings and sensations of their body. With stress and overwhelm come numbness, maladaptive coping mechanisms, and disconnection. We get permanently stuck in "go" mode and lose connection to the effortlessness of "flow" of feeling.

When we "get into our heads," and get stuck in "go" mode, meaning when we prioritize thinking and doing over feeling and being—the "flow" mode—our thoughts and actions have a compulsive quality. Once we are in the mindset of getting things done, it is not easy to get back to the relaxed, open state of flowing naturally. Even if we know intellectually that we should slow down, the energetics in our body might not cooperate.

....

Once we are in the mindset of getting things done, it is
not easy to get back to the relaxed, open state of flowing
naturally. Even if we know intellectually that we should slow
down, the energetics in our body might not cooperate.

....

So how do we escape the seemingly inevitable reality of disconnection and stress, and their effects on our bodies, without giving up the ability to be successful and productive?

As we reclaim our natural state of aliveness and pleasure, the area to consider first and foremost is our body.

Since vitality and sensual sensations happen in and through the body, trying to think our way into them is like trying to think our way into riding a bicycle. Reading books on bicycle riding and talking about bicycle riding do not translate into sitting on a bike and knowing how to ride.

Thinking and talking about reclaiming your pleasure is a great first step, but does not necessarily translate into having the bodily wherewithal to open, soften, and relax. Physical closures, contractions, and habits are acquired through repetition in the body and can be undone by consciously practicing new patterns within your body and nervous system.

As humans, we learn through repetition. Every activity is wired into the body-mind through repeating an activity. When we learn something new, our whole system interconnects. What first felt foreign and almost impossible to do, over time and repetition becomes the pattern we use automatically.

All patterns have somatic, emotional, and mental components. Once a pattern has been learned, it is accessed automatically and becomes second nature. One important fact to keep in mind is that the body does not make a differentiation between "helpful" and "detrimental" patterns. It simply repeats what it has been programmed to do through repetition.

There are two parallel approaches we will consider in this chapter: 1) Understanding the dynamics of the body in order to release programming that is no longer useful, and 2) relaxing the body enough to regain its inborn feminine genius.

A Woman's Energetic Body

Even though each woman is built as a unique expression, with her own physiological and psychological makeup, and our personal histories and programming determine how we each relate to our bodies, there are some principles that apply to all of us.

I am giving you an overview and an energetic map here so you can explore your particular relationship to your own body within a framework I call "Energy Distribution," which teaches us to pay attention to how our life-force energy is distributed within our body at any given time. In section IV: "Sacred Practices of the Wild Woman," pp. 197–236, you will find many practical exercises and applications that you can use once you understand these principles.

We begin with your relationship to your own body. Before we can connect with and feel others, we need to become sensitive to and educated about our own energetic dynamics. Once you understand your own reasons for any numbness, tension, and strain that you may carry in your body, you can easily undo the related habitual body patterns and restore yourself to a state of pleasurable aliveness and sensual well-being.

....

Once you understand your own reasons for any numbness, tension, and strain that you may carry in your body, you can easily undo the related habitual body patterns and restore yourself to a state of pleasurable aliveness and sensual well-being.

....

Creation and Power

As we engage with our energetic bodies, the first aspect to consider is that we as women are built for procreation as a means of perpetuating the survival of our species. Our bodies are made to conceive, carry a child, and give birth. We are capable of feeding a baby with our own bodies, and our bodies bleed and replenish every month. In order to fulfill our biological functions (whether we choose to have children or not), we need energy in the lower body.

This life-force not only allows us to create human life, but also is the origin of power, creativity, nurturing, and beauty in our world.

The natural seat of energy in our bodies is low in the hips, thighs, genitals, and belly. Our native body movements are nonlinear, undulating, swirling, and full. When our lower bodies are engaged, we have access to our natural wisdom, feelings, intuition, and abundant creativity. True, raw power, strength, and intuition are all available to each of us through our lower bodies.

> When our lower bodies are engaged, we have access to our natural wisdom, feelings, intuition, and abundant creativity. True, raw power, strength, and intuition are all available to each of us through our lower bodies.

When we look at images of women in indigenous cultures, we often see them squatting together close to the ground, cooking, sharing stories, or dancing in a way that actively engages their hips and thighs. Those kinds of activities, all of them connected to the earth, are a source of nurturing, communion, and creative momentum, and are essential for our well-being. Reconnecting with our original, earth-infused vitality can be done with something as simple as gathering with other women or allowing time for creative expression and dance.

That said, most of us spend our day far from such simple activities. Instead we are:

Stuck in "Go" Mode

Most of us are very busy "doing" and thinking. We work on computers, spend our time texting or browsing, posting or commenting on social media, immersed in our minds. All the while, we are parking our bodies in chairs, cars, and public transport. We direct others, get stuff done, and tick off endless to-do lists.

Most women I work with complain of chronic tension, tight necks and shoulders, clenched jaws, and headaches. They report a lack of desire, an array of hormonal and stress-related issues, and a disconnection from themselves, their feelings, and their true power and sensual pleasure.

This is not to say we have to get rid of our smartphones, or attempt to escape modern life and return to a tribal existence. Our "doing" and "being" aspects can both be defined, learned, integrated, and then applied as a choice. This empowers us to have both a rich feminine creative expression and the ability to be effective in business and work.

....

Our "doing" and "being" aspects can both be defined,
learned, integrated, and then applied as a choice.

....

When we understand our bodies' energetic patterns, we can remedy stress and fluidly switch between the modalities of "flow" and "go."

> When we understand our bodies' energetic patterns,
> we can remedy stress and fluidly switch between
> the modalities of "flow" and "go."

Energetically, for most women, the act of "doing" means that we have to apply different mechanics that are less natural to our bodies. Applying direction and focus, implementing a plan, creating forward motion, following a schedule, and engaging in strong mental activity all necessitate a different way of harnessing energy.

To be effective in the world, physically as well as intellectually, we have to gather all our energy, squeeze it upward with our core, and then harness it for forward action. If you pay attention to the mechanics of this, you can feel the tightening of your core and the upward movement that takes place as you gather momentum for "doing."

These particular actions cause tension in a woman's body. If the action is correlated with emotional stress, we develop the mental and physical habit of tightening and tensing while "doing." The pattern becomes ingrained, and every time we enter "doing," the activity reloads the stress and tension felt previously. Over time, our muscles, organs, tissues, and ligaments—and our nervous system—will carry a certain kind of habitual contraction and "push."

Instead of the spiraling, undulating, wide motion that is our native energetic disposition, we train ourselves to gather our energy and squeeze it upward toward the thinking and doing centers of our head. It often gets stuck there, creating tension in the neck, shoulders, jaw, and head.

From that state of tension, we become disconnected from the lower body and its innate wisdom and feeling. Training ourselves to "get things done" is not the issue in itself.

As mentioned earlier, our bodies learn through repetition. The more we repeat an activity, the more it becomes the "default" setting. Over time we lose the "muscle" of our inborn energetics and are no longer able to access them easily. At that point, we are unable to soften toward our partners, or ourselves, in a fluid way. We become stuck, less creative, less sensual, disconnected, and insensitive, and in turn, that perpetuates the cycle of head-driven "doing" and the associated physical and emotional complaints.

Often, we feel so numb and disconnected from our bodies that the endeavors of feeling our partners or reaching an aroused state feel too daunting to even try.

Reclaiming "Flow"

Once you understand these dynamics, it is possible to counteract the vicious cycle. The same way we never forget the first language we learn to speak, we never forget the sensual, alive, feminine flow for which we are built.

There are two main strategies to counteract this habitual upward squeeze: Nonlinear, Unstructured, Free Movement; and Lower Body Relaxation—both described below.

Nonlinear, Unstructured, Free Movement

How often do you engage in unstructured bodily activity? Do you jump up and down, flail your arms wildly, roll on the ground, dance as if no one is watching, make sounds, and let yourself be moved by your feelings?

The quickest way to counteract the patterns of "push" and upward motion is to do the exact opposite. Many of us practice yoga, lift weights, run, or cycle as ways to combat stress and sitting. These are all valuable activities, and any way the body is activated, within reason, provides health benefits. However, all of these activities follow a structure, which once again habituates the body to more linear patterns.

The key is to break out of linear activity and re-wild your nervous system into what is native to your body. Here is one of the simplest and most effective exercises I give to my students and practice myself. This practice is also described in the section IV: "Sacred Practices of the Wild Woman," pp. 197–236, as the "The Wild Woman's Foundational Practice," (found below) along with a few other exercises to return your energetic self to its natural flow.

The Wild Woman's Foundational Practice:
Moving What You Are Feeling

Put on a piece of music. Ideally, pick one that has a good beat and no lyrics. Begin by just standing. Feel your feet on the ground and mentally give yourself this time for yourself.

Begin moving your body to follow whatever you are feeling. If you feel stress, move as stress. If you feel numb, move as numbness. This is not a dance, there is no need to look good or even feel good; this is an exploration into how your body wants to move when given permission to do so. You'll notice that as you move with one sensation, the next sensation will arise and you will begin moving with that sensation or feeling.

Don't follow the impulse to use structured dance moves; don't even attempt to move with the rhythm. Just allow whatever your body feels to be translated into motion. Sounds might happen, emotions will come and go, or perhaps you will feel nothing, which is also fine; just keep on moving with whatever shows up.

Do this with at least one song every day, and you will experience the slow unwinding of your system, and the reconnection to your natural disposition. If you have more time, do more, but keep in mind that for the body to repattern, a short time of daily practice is better than one long stretch of practice done once a week.

Now that you know something of the energetics of a woman's body and how to counteract established patterns, you can begin to incorporate moments of nonlinear activity into your daily life. This can be in the form of this exercise, or by playing with your children or pets. You can wiggle in your car, shake out your body in the shower, or undulate your hips while washing the dishes. I invite you to experiment with how much unstructured motion you can bring into your day.

Lower Body Relaxation

For a moment, turn your attention to the base of your body. If you are seated, feel where your body meets the chair. Notice the quality of muscular activity. Are your buttocks clenched? Do you have tension in your pelvic floor? Can you feel sensations in your genitals? Is your energy pulled up and in?

Without changing anything, take a snapshot of the muscular tension and any feeling that comes with it. Then, focus on the area with the most tension, and slowly start tensing that area even more. You might be able to isolate the muscles involved, or you might just tighten the whole pelvic region a bit more. Squeeze and tighten as you inhale for a moment, then exhale and relax as much as you can.

Notice the sensations as you relax. Based on what you observe, begin to bring your attention toward relaxing the lower body. Once again, you can do this almost anytime and anywhere.

Tightness in our feminine power center—the lower body—not only hinders the flow of blood to our vital organs but it also cuts off our feelings, sensations, and native wisdom. By bringing attention to your muscular contractions and dissolving habitual muscle clench, you will gain agency over the dynamics of tension and release.

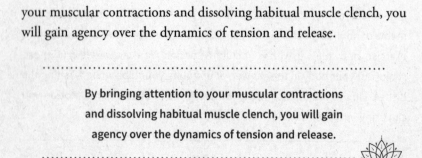

> By bringing attention to your muscular contractions and dissolving habitual muscle clench, you will gain agency over the dynamics of tension and release.

You will be able to choose when to tighten the body to get things done and when to relax and flow. Over time, you will learn how to use only the tension necessary to get things done and separate the emotional strands from the physical necessities. You'll have access to your full range of ability and expression, switching back and forth between "doing" and "being."

6

Embodiment

THAO IS A FORCE OF NATURE. DEDICATED AND DISCIPLINED, SHE PURSUES anything she starts with great vigor and curiosity. She is also incredibly generous and deeply social. She is a member of our advanced women's study group in Amsterdam, and her inspiring story posts help to motivate the other women in her group to explore the practices.

Thao was born in Vietnam and was an infant when her parents fled with her by boat. The family settled in Australia, where she was raised and educated. Today, she spends her time working in both Bali and Europe.

When I first met her, she described herself as ambitious, extremely hardworking, and driven to succeed. However, she mentioned that she had started having anxiety attacks a year earlier, as she found herself "in between jobs, in between homes, in between countries, in between lives." Her goal was to learn how to get out of her head, calm her body and mind, and find out what she wanted for her life.

She started with the Wild Woman's Foundational Practices and soon began to explore Non-Linear Movement® as a daily practice as a way to engage with her feelings and bodily sensations. With the movement came awareness of areas of unresolved experiences, all the way back to the first months of her life. Over the years, she has explored many of the practices outlined in this book and is now immersing in the more advanced Deity Yoga practice of my lineage.

Recently, she tagged me in this Facebook post:

HOW I WENT FROM RUNNING 5K TO 10K IN 6 DAYS

If you have known me for a long time, you'll know how hilarious and borderline ridiculous the title of this post is! I've always hated exercise, and in the past, I've had zero discipline. I find it uninteresting, boring, and it hurts.

And yet here I am, at 38, discovering I might actually like running. Instead of thinking of running as exercise, I changed it into an embodiment practice that focuses on relaxing and sensitizing my body.

I started by running two minutes and walking ninety seconds (repeat and rotate). I did this for two weeks, and then, one day, I just started to run. On my first run, I ran 5K nonstop. Six days later I ran 10K. And now I'm up to 15K!

Here's how I did it.

1. Firstly, I aim to exercise at 70% of my capacity (something Steve James and Michaela Boehm taught me). I do this because at 70% I can still maintain sensitivity and feel sensations in my body.

2. I'll run as fast as I can while still feeling my body and being as relaxed as possible. If I can't feel my body, I'll slow down until I can feel it. My progress is based on how fast I can run while still being relaxed.

3. I don't focus on my breathing . . . Instead, you guessed it . . . I focus on feeling my body. There are a few ways I do this:

(i) Sometimes I do a body scan and see where my body is tense . . . I'll intensify the tenseness for a moment and then release it (while still running).

(ii) Sometimes I imagine water moving horizontally across/through my body as though I'm in a lake. I do this to counteract the forward push motion of the running. This slows me down to feel my body. I love doing this if my hips or chest are tight. Strangely, when I do this, my heart rate goes up, and I run faster.

By running this way, I change my experience from fitness/exercise to an "embodiment practice" that aligns with my personal values. My personal belief is that the more I sensitize and feel my body, the easier I can navigate the world and the more I can trust myself.

4. After my run, I do Michaela's "Non-Linear Movement Method®" to counteract the forward motion of the running. I play about 2–3 songs and allow my body to stretch and move any which way it wants. I think this step is crucial because it softens my body and makes the recovery smooth. So far I've had zero pain or soreness in my body despite running for up to 15k.

I'm not looking for a "success formula" to help me run better. I wake up thinking, what can I feel today? So far, I've explored running from my pelvis, running from my cervix, feeling my muscles fall away from my bones when I'm running (it was heavenly, I've even explored running from my fascia. It's very interesting and super-exciting).

This post summarizes accurately what happens when we listen to our bodies. What Thao describes in her post is the result of full embodiment. Through relaxing and sensitizing, she was able to perceive sensations and feelings in her body and also to learn to trust what she is feeling. This, in turn, led to her being able to track her body's signals and adjust accordingly.

Thao's transformation has been incredible to watch. Not only is she running and taking care of her body, she is also free from anxiety. She reports that the embodiment practices have not only given her access to the wisdom of her body, but also the ability to feel and interact with others. By listening to herself, she learned how to listen to others. She now runs her own business in a highly creative field and uses her ability to feel and listen in her work with her clients.

What Is Embodiment?

"Embodiment" has become a much-used buzzword as somatic therapies have become more widely used and accepted. Somatic modalities take us beyond "talk therapy" to engage our whole being. Somatic Experiencing®, for example, created by trauma therapist Peter A. Levine, PhD, (author of *In an Unspoken Voice: How the Body Releases Trauma and Restores Goodness*) helps us to release trauma by tracking bodily sensations that correspond with our thoughts and emotions. As we pay attention to these tangible sensations, they shift, migrate, and transform within the body, opening the way for a corresponding transformation of our mental and emotional states.

For the longest time, most psychotherapy modalities only concerned themselves with the cognitive processing of events, trauma, and family interactions. It was considered that talking about things would allow people to process and put the events in their proper place. How those issues influenced the body and how the body informed the person's view of the issues were not a priority in treatment.

Pioneers like Dr. Levine and Bessel van der Kolk, MD, (author of *The Body Keeps the Score*) have contributed significantly to a more holistic approach to the treatment of mind and body. Somatic therapies have changed the way we treat trauma of all kinds and brought awareness of how emotional and mental events affect the body. Most importantly, there is now widespread understanding of how the body stores trauma and unexamined or unfinished emotional material, and how the psyche moves away from the body until the trauma is released or resolved. Dr. van der Kolk's research shows that trauma actually re-shapes the body and the brain, limiting our ability to engage socially, to trust, to exercise self-control, and to experience pleasure. These can be restored through neurofeedback and embodiment practices such as sports, art therapy, or unstructured movement.

In this context, the term "embodiment" can be understood to mean "coming back into the body." Of course, as long as we are alive, we are always in our bodies. But that does not mean we are aware of what is happening in our bodies. Embodiment is the process of becoming alive to the signals of our bodies. The awareness of the signals of the body can also be described as sensual recognition. Being with the full array of sensory and emotional perception—the sublime as well as the ugly—allows us to savor the full human experience: body, mind, and spirit; alive, open, and integrated.

....

Being with the full array of sensory and emotional perception—the sublime as well as the ugly—allows us to savor the full human experience: body, mind, and spirit; alive, open, and integrated.

....

Why We Disembody

Depending on how much mental activity, stress, overwhelm, or trauma we experience, we might lose awareness of sensations in our bodies. This state can be anything from mild numbness all the way to full-blown disconnection and disembodiment.

In psychology, the term for this is "dissociation," which describes a wide array of experiences, ranging from mild detachment from our immediate surroundings to more severe detachment from bodily and emotional experience. In mild cases, it can be regarded as a coping mechanism in attempting to manage, minimize, or tolerate stress—including boredom or conflict. In more extreme cases, we almost completely lose touch with what we are feeling. We will discuss these mechanisms in more detail in the next chapter, chapter 7, "Barriers to Embodiment," pp. 183–97.

Most of us have experienced the loss of connection with the body while working intensely on a computer. Because the body is essentially "parked" in a chair and the mind is focused on a task that's intensely cerebral, we might not notice bad posture, thirst, or aches in the body. Often, it is only when we stand up that we become aware of how little we felt while engaged.

> Most of us have experienced the loss of connection with the body while working intensely on a computer. Because the body is essentially "parked" in a chair and the mind is focused on a task that's intensely cerebral, we might not notice bad posture, thirst, or aches in the body.

Mental activity can focus our awareness such that the body's signs and signals are no longer perceived. Triggers from previous trauma—everything from physical injury to emotional hurt to traumatic events—make us escape potentially painful sensations by numbing us to the sensations felt in the body. A tried-and-true numbing mechanism most of us have employed is eating a pint of ice cream while watching a movie as a means of not having to feel the fullness of a stressful work situation or breakup. We use substances like ice cream, rich foods, or alcohol to drown out the signals of distress our emotional body is sending us.

Overwhelm of any kind can drown out the signals of the body in the same way that loud noises drown out the quieter ones. In all these instances, we are disconnected from the body's signs and sensations and, with that, we lose touch with the body's natural ability to feel an environment and judge situations accurately.

My coteacher, Steve James, often says to imagine the noise of the stress, overwhelm, and trauma to be like a loud band playing a live concert. Your friend next to you is screaming in your ear, trying to communicate, yet you can barely hear what he or she is saying. If you were suddenly transported into a serene library, your friend's voice would be perceived as loud, crazy screaming. Your friend's voice is the voice of your body, and the environment determines how much of the message you can hear.

What Embodiment Is Not

Sometimes embodiment is confused with generating strong stimuli in order to feel something, which is not the same. In fact, certain types of vigorous activity can produce strong reactions in the body which in turn can also drown out subtler sensations and signals. For example, if you go straight from your stressful job to a high-intensity spinning class, you will leave class with your body buzzing. However, the buzzing is a sign of an overtaxed nervous system and drowns out the signals of fatigue and potential physical misalignment.

The key here is to become familiar with your body and how much movement and sensory engagement is right for you. Refraining from pushing your body to the maximum has many benefits, among them the ability to feel subtle sensations. Steve James emphasizes this in his embodiment teachings, which is what Thao refers to in her post as the "70%." This is the idea that by engaging only 70 percent of your practice capacity, you retain your fine-feeling sensitivity so that you can feel how your body is responding in real time.

For instance, you may become aware of a certain numbness to sensations in your body and start doing yoga to come back into your body. As you engage in vigorous stretching, you can feel the strong sensations in your hamstrings, which are way louder than the subtle sensations of strain in your lower back as it gets taxed in the process. It is not until later, when the strong feelings in the hamstrings have subsided, that you can feel the pain in your lower back.

Our practice must be done in such a way that our feeling connection to the body is not severed. Otherwise, we not only lose out on the valuable education process of getting to know our bodies and minds but we also miss injury as it occurs in the moment, only to notice it in the aftermath when it's too late.

> Our practice must be done in such a way that our feeling connection to the body is not severed. Otherwise, we not only lose out on the valuable education process of getting to know our bodies and minds but we also miss injury as it occurs in the moment, only to notice it in the aftermath when it's too late.

The Natural Genius of the Body

The body has its own wisdom and systems of navigation, honed by survival as our species developed over millions of years. Not only do we each have an advanced predator warning system deeply embedded in our perception, but we also have an intricate nervous system that enables us to go from rest to flight in mere seconds. Our "Spidey senses" are much more effective than any conscious cognitive function.

Even though we have lost access to many of those fine perceptions, they are still as present as ever, and we use them without knowing. For instance, most people will still perceive it when someone stares at their back. Being observed from behind is one of the oldest threats humans have faced. Walking around and being watched by a stealthy predator about to attack was a reality for much of the evolution of humankind.

Try focusing your attention by looking intently at the back of someone's neck. He or she might not know why but will turn around and look. Only the person who is totally distracted or numb will no longer sense the potential threat. For most of us, the body is still an instrument of finely tuned feeling.

Embodiment Practices

Sensitizing and relaxing go hand in hand here. By relaxing the nervous system, we lower the noise level so we can once again perceive the signals the body sends. By sensitizing ourselves to pick up those signals, we avail ourselves of ancient wisdom within our bodies.

Bringing awareness into the lower half of our bodies is particularly beneficial, since it not only enlivens the body but also sensitizes us to the pleasure and power we carry in our hips and pelvis.

Hip Circles

Stand barefoot with your feet hip-width apart. Bring your hands onto your hips and begin to make circles with your hips. Start out with small, subtle motions and widen the motion only as your hips awaken to the movement. The key here is not to force your body to open faster than it wants to. Particularly since we sit for long periods of time, it is important not to "wrench" the hips open. As your hips awaken, you can experiment with different motions.

Try going faster or slower than you normally would. Move your hips in figure eights, and if you feel like having fun, try writing your name with your hip movements. Make sure your feet are solidly planted on the ground. When you are ready to finish, make the movements gradually subtler until you come to complete stillness. Stand with your eyes closed and feel your body.

Notice all the different sensations within your body. Where does your body feel pleasurable and alive? What areas of the body feel tight? What emotions can you feel as you stand quietly?

Once we can feel our bodies again, we have ready access to what I call "background" sensations. Those sensations range from subtle joint or neck pains to stress signs such as heightened pulse and dull headaches, which signal overwhelm or danger long before we have a breakdown or find ourselves in a tricky situation, to feelings of pleasant aliveness, which aid greatly in a more sensual and alive relationship with the body. Background sensations also play a major part in intuition and intimacy. Intuition translates the subtle signs the body perceives from the environment and people around us into the cognitive realm. The more we can feel, the more information we receive. The same is true for intimacy. We feel our partners via the sensations we perceive in our own body. The more we are connected to ourselves, the better we can feel and connect with our partners.

....

Intuition translates the subtle signs the body perceives from the environment and people around us into the cognitive realm. The more we can feel, the more information we receive.

....

In a broader sense, embodiment practices and considerations can lead to what I call "Feminine Embodiment." When you can listen and perceive with your body, mind, and heart, your natural expression of who you are as a woman can be heard and, with the help of an open body, expressed fully. As you care equally for your body and your mind, your spirit can express itself freely. All sensations and emotions are being taken into account, and you can express yourself fully as the glorious woman you truly are.

When I look at Thao in the picture she posted with her running story—windswept hair under a cap, rosy face and proud, sparkling eyes—I see a woman who is alive, no longer bound by the restrictions of her anxious mind or her cultural conditioning. I am proud of her and know that this translates into her life and work and how she inspires others—men and woman alike—to engage not only with the head but with the entire being.

7

Barriers to Embodiment

FOR THE SAKE OF CREATING A FULLER UNDERSTANDING OF EMBODIMENT, this chapter covers the most common barriers to it. Here are the top three reasons why we lose contact with feeling in our bodies, have a diminished experience of pleasure, and lack access to our intuition and bodily intelligence:

Stress and Anxiety
Overwhelm
Trauma

Stress and Anxiety

Considering the demands of modern life, for most women stress is a constant companion. In its most extreme form, stress leads to anxiety, both situational anxiety, spiking when extra stressors, such as deadlines, a near traffic collision, or a fight with our partner occur, and chronic anxiety, as when a high stress load becomes constant for a length of time. The mechanisms of stress in the body reduce our ability to feel our body and the messages it sends.

The reason for this comes from the way our bodies developed to survive. The body does not know the difference between an actual and a perceived threat. Back in the early days of humankind, survival was our number one priority. Finding food, procreating, and staying alive took much of our available energy.

Imagine you are living in a cave; you just had food after a hunt and are resting when suddenly you hear rustling outside. Immediately, all your faculties come online and your body goes from a state of deep relaxation into full-blown alertness. If an actual predator appeared in the cave, your fight-or-flight instinct would kick in rapidly.

When this happens, your body takes over and adrenaline is released into the bloodstream, causing a cascade of physiological responses designed to give you the best chance of survival. Your heartbeat speeds up and your breathing accelerates, delivering extra oxygen to your entire system, and your eyes focus only on what is right in front of you.

Your cognitive function is greatly diminished, since thinking about what to do would take too long. Instinct takes over, and your body fights or flees as quickly as possible. If you survive, your body has a certain set of built-in responses to release you from the experience—mainly trembling and shaking until your nervous system is reset—and then you go back to living your life.

This fight-or-flight response is meant to be followed by the body's mechanisms for release, which reset the entire body after the threat has passed. Both the fight-or-flight response and the subsequent release process are necessary for survival and for optimal physical condition.

This is true for humans as well as for animals, and we will explore the release aspect a bit further on in this chapter when I discuss trauma (pp. 92–97).

This effective mechanism was gradually disrupted as our lives and relationship to the natural world shifted so that most of the daily "threats" we experience are not actual physical threats.

There is no actual threat to your life in the moment you see a car collision on TV. You are not in bodily danger when a work deadline is suddenly sprung on you. You generally don't need to fight for your survival when someone honks at you in traffic, and you are not being expelled from the tribe if you say the wrong thing in a meeting.

However, your body does not know this and reacts similarly to the way it would if you were facing a saber-toothed cat. Because the body does not know the difference between perceived and actual threat to your life, the nervous system, which controls how you react to danger for the sake of survival, goes into stress response. With an overwhelming amount of perceived threats, the response becomes constant.

The sympathetic nervous system, which is responsible for fight-or-flight, is one part of our autonomic nervous system. Many people living under stressful life conditions experience the bodily effects of constant background fight-or-flight responses. Conflicts at work, a difficult commute, and the day-to-day strains of paying the bills and meeting obligations all create stress. In the extreme, this accumulation of low-level fight-or-flight responses bathes the body in stress hormones for such a prolonged period that it can develop into panic attacks and other health problems.

When I was a therapist in private practice, I found a simple way of explaining panic attacks to my clients, which were all too common among them.

I asked them to imagine that within their body they had a cup that collected stress responses. Every time a stress stimulus was present, it was like a drop dripping into the cup. Every perceived or real threat, both mental and physical, would produce drops. This meant that everything from negative self-talk, to worrying, to watching violence on TV, to swerving to avoid hitting another car all contributed to the liquid rising in the cup.

In the course of a stressful day the cup would fill up. I explained that by about fifty percent capacity, they would start experiencing real stress, and when the cup overflowed it resulted in a panic attack, which is the body's classic fight-or-flight response.

The symptoms of a panic attack are the same symptoms you would have if a saber-toothed cat were at your cave entrance. Some of the more commonly described symptoms of a panic attack are:

- Hyperventilation, which is precipitated by the need for extra oxygen to power the body
- Increased heart rate and blood pressure
- Tunnel vision, which aids in getting focused on only the threat at hand
- Numbness or tingling in the extremities as blood is rushed to the areas of the body needed to fight or run
- Sweating and/or chills from the adrenaline
- A sense of terror and impending doom; fear of death
- Nauseous feeling in the stomach, which results from the adrenaline surge

These responses come in handy if you need to find a club and hit some huge hairy beast over the head. They are rather inconvenient if, let's say, you have had a stressful day and are now rushing to get ready for travel. You are finally on the plane, settling in, when suddenly the plane hits a turbulence bump, which contributes the final drops to your already brimming cup.

Suddenly, you are having a panic attack on a plane, which then, of course, makes you think you now have a flying phobia, which was always right under the surface but would not have produced such an extreme response if your cup were emptier.

Then, the next time you get on a plane, you start worrying about having another panic attack, which produces more drips in the cup. In the worst-case scenario, you have a panic attack before you even get on the plane.

This used to be my simple explanation to my clients, which ended in my describing and teaching them the following ways to "empty the cup":

Sleep is the most effective way to empty the cup. By design, the body repairs and recovers during sleep, with many functions contributing to rest and reset. Many of us don't sleep nearly enough, either because we have young children or work long hours, or we have jet lag or are experiencing chronic stress or sensory overload. Getting seven to eight hours of quality sleep per night has wide-ranging health benefits, including healthy brain function, emotional well-being, optimal performance, and overall health. The best practices for sleep require a gradual step down from high activity to actual sleep, and with it a gradual reducing of blue light (as in TV and phone screens). I see this as a great opportunity for engagement with our sensual side! Instead of checking social media up to the point of turning the lights off, light a candle, enjoy a bath, have a hot or cold drink you truly savor, listen to some music, spend time caring lovingly for your body, and engage in pleasurable activities that prepare you for sleep.

Meditation calms the mind and benefits cardiovascular and immune function, reduces stress, and improves concentration. Meditating does not need to be a daunting task that requires perfect spinal posture and pretzel-like legs. Simply sit quietly for five or ten minutes, perhaps with a cup of tea. Turn your phone off, close the door, and just let yourself be. No need for any special technique; just sit quietly. Your mind will begin to unwind, which most likely will result in more thinking for a moment, instead of less. If you can just sit and rest your body while this happens, you'll eventually feel a sense of ease. The important aspect is to not force the mind or body at all. Just sit, and all else will happen in its own time.

Movement has immense benefits for the whole body by increasing breath circulation as well as blood and lymph flow. It also reduces anxiety by making the fight-or-flight system less reactive. Our bodies are built to move, and they respond to movement with increased well-being. If you are looking to reduce anxiety and at the same time engage with your body in a sensual way, dance vigorously around the house. There can't be enough said about the power of moving our hips, engaging our thighs, and letting ourselves enjoy rhythm and flow. The good thing about all these "emptying the cup" practices is that they double as engagement with our sensual selves. If you are prone to persistent anxiety or have trauma in your body, consider getting a small rebounder and jumping on it a few times a day. In somatic therapies, this has been proven to reduce trauma-related symptoms and, in addition, it's great fun!

....

> Our bodies are built to move, and they respond to movement with increased well-being. If you are looking to reduce anxiety and at the same time engage with your body in a sensual way, dance vigorously around the house. There can't be enough said about the power of moving our hips, engaging our thighs, and letting ourselves enjoy rhythm and flow.

....

Creativity and ritual engage the creative part of our brain as well as inspire us to feel beyond ourselves. One of my personal favorite ways of using creativity to reduce stress is coloring. To me, every aspect of coloring has stress-relieving as well as sensual benefits. I choose coloring books with themes I specifically want to engage with. The books could contain illustrations or designs of deities, stylized plants, or calming mandalas. I own several sets of coloring pencils and buy extra ones in the colors I love the most. Just looking at the pencils gives me joy and stimulates my creative imagination. Coloring has the added benefit of having the boundaries of one's creativity defined via the outlines, so there is no effort involved. I can simply flow with choosing colors and enjoy the theme I am filling in. I have found that coloring while on a plane tremendously reduces my occasional turbulence-induced flight anxiety and fills the time in a more beneficial way than watching a movie.

Attend to patterns of negative thinking and self-talk. This can be done by focusing on positive affirmations as well as through cognitive behavioral changes and reframing. Much has been written about manifesting and creating fantastic outcomes through crafting just the right words, but for myself and my clients, I prefer to focus on very simple, practical sentences that support the current situation. My teacher instructed me in chanting mantras, which are a quintessential part of Deity Yoga practice, and I noticed over time that when I spoke a mantra that I had previously had positive engagement with, it allowed me to enter a positive state instantly.

Based on this principle of positive association, and the knowledge that repetition creates new pathways in the brain, I suggest that you find a few short sentences that function as both praise and affirmation. Think about how you would speak to a small child to encourage him or her, and use that tone and kindness for your own affirmations.

Make sure you have a mantra of praise for yourself after you have successfully mastered a stressful moment. For instance, if you are anxious about a task, you can repeat the mantras of "I can do this," "I am fine, it's going to be OK," and then when you have completed the task, praise yourself by repeating, "See, you did great!" or "You did a good job!" This sounds very simplistic, but by repeating short, praise-oriented phrases, you are speaking with yourself the way others who love you would speak to you, which has additional benefits in the realm of self-love and care. Over time, the positive associations via previous successes will immediately bring you into a positive state when you speak your chosen affirmation.

By emptying the cup in all of these ways, we allow our parasympathetic nervous system—the other part of our autonomic system—to activate and prevent high-stress and panic situations. The parasympathetic nervous system's responses, often called "Rest and Digest," or "Feed and Breed," work together with the sympathetic nervous system to regulate the whole body, and both are always needed. Even if you are deeply relaxed, the sympathetic nervous system stays alert. Both are involved in creating homeostasis, which is the body's ability to heal and calm itself.

Activating the parasympathetic nervous system allows for embodiment. By necessity, the fight-or-flight response cuts out your awareness of your body, because in a survival state, the feelings and sensations of the body are inconsequential and potentially distracting.

You will find further fun exercises and useful practices for all aspects of emptying the cup in section IV: "Sacred Practices of the Wild Woman," pp. 197–236.

Overload

Overload, as the word describes perfectly, is when our system experiences "too much" and can no longer process or cope with the excess stimulus. The toll on our system produces a similar physiological response to that of stress.

The source of the "too much" can be external, which is common in this busy world; e-mails, phone calls, texts, social media, exposure to noise, traffic, and crowds are all a daily occurrence for most of us.

The sense of "too much" also comes from an internal source; excess thinking or emotional drama and any kind of internal loop in your mind all contribute to the state of overwhelm. This is particularly true when you are working while sitting still. Because you park your body, all the energy goes toward mental activity. By definition, you are disembodied, meaning you are not paying attention to the signals your body sends.

This excess stimulation leads to all the bodily energy going upward toward the head. This leads to a number of disembodying factors and symptoms:

- Tight neck, tight shoulders, clenched jaw, and headaches
- Contracted pelvic floor, tension in the genitals, and tension in the layers of the pelvic bowl
- Tight buttocks and thighs
- Tension in the belly
- Tension in the breath or shallow breathing in the upper chest, which signals the body to adopt a panic response

When the overload is ongoing, it can lead to heightened pulse, higher blood pressure, and chronic tension. With too much noise, the signals of our body are drowned out. (The signals are always there—you just can't hear them.)

You might have had the experience of not paying attention to your body during high-input, high-stress times and feeling basically fine. Then, when you rest or perhaps even get a massage, you are suddenly aching and tense. The fact is, you felt like this all along but could not feel it, as you were numb to the messages of your body.

When we are brought back in touch with the signals of our body, the sensations are often heightened because suddenly they are front and center.

Tension, stress, overload, and anxiety responses cause specific coping patterns in the body that are different for each person. Those particular neuromuscular patterns form an armor, a layer of tension in the body that, over time, becomes chronic and creates a permanent barrier to embodiment.

The ultimate remedy to overload is obviously to reduce the stimuli, both external and internal. Certain inflow can't be stopped, since we live in a communal environment, but there are some easy reductions that can be made:

- Reducing our time on e-mail, computer, and phone
- Limiting our social media engagement
- Turning off the TV running in the background

- Driving in silence instead of listening to the radio
- Reducing mental chatter and emotional upheaval by learning mindfulness techniques
- Engaging in somatic processes that release pent-up emotions

Small changes that accumulate over time will make a substantial difference in your system. You will find overload reduction exercises and suggestions in section IV: "Sacred Practices of the Wild Woman," pp. 197–236.

Trauma

To understand embodiment, it is relevant to understand how the body responds to and remembers trauma. Often, when we first reconnect with our bodies, what we come in touch with are sensations and emotions that are not pleasant. Memories and injuries are stored in the body, and when we begin to listen to the signals of our body, old unresolved trauma can surface.

Trauma and trauma responses are common barriers to feeling and pleasure in the body. They can range from mild discomfort and an unwillingness to feel, all the way to debilitating emotions and, in extreme cases, severe distress and inability to function.

> Trauma and trauma responses are common barriers to feeling and pleasure in the body. They can range from mild discomfort and an unwillingness to feel, all the way to debilitating emotions and, in extreme cases, severe distress and inability to function.

I am defining trauma here broadly, spanning everything from bodily injury to severe physical and sexual trauma. Living in the world means that, at some point, every human being will experience trauma of some kind.

As I mentioned earlier, our body is naturally equipped to release trauma. You might have experienced a version of it yourself. After a traumatic event, the body shakes and shivers. With the shaking might come emotional release, as well as crying. If we allow this process to come to an end naturally, without stopping or suppressing it, the after-effects leave the body and we don't store the event in our body-mind.

You might have seen this in the animal kingdom. If you ever have watched a National Geographic program, you will have seen the classic scenario of a prey animal, such as a gazelle, being chased by a predator, perhaps a cheetah. Every so often you will see the prey escaping. The documentary will then show the animal standing, shaking and shivering. Then, at some point, the gazelle does one final shake, almost like a dog shaking off water, and just walks off, starts eating, and joins the herd.

This is similar to the way humans naturally deal with trauma. Unfortunately, this process is often suppressed by the necessity to deal with the aftereffects of an event, or through other circumstances. Medically, after surgery, the body is often kept from trembling or shaking in order to release trauma, since the benefits of somatic release are still not widely known, and shaking could pose risks to a fresh incision. More often than not, we "suck it up," or we are the victims of circumstances in which we are so helpless that we can't access our body at all.

Dr. Peter A. Levine, a pioneer in the field of somatic trauma treatment, details his own traumatic injury, recovery, and subsequent findings in his book, *In an Unspoken Voice: How the Body Releases Trauma and Restores Goodness.*[5] Dr. Levine's books are absolute must-reads if you would like to understand the effects of traumatic events on your body and life.

If you have experienced substantial bodily, emotional, or sexual trauma, I strongly recommend that you work with a qualified trauma therapist. Dr. Levine has trained and certified many qualified professionals. You will find his information in the Resources section on p. 241.

If your body is not able to process whatever trauma you have experienced, it will get stuck and create a neuromuscular pattern of bodily contraction. This pattern will have all the information of the event, plus your fear or defense response, and any bodily sensations. A similar event, or emotional or bodily sensation, can trigger the pattern and reawaken the trauma response.

This is important to know, as these sensations are unprocessed and usually so strong that the body shuts off. It becomes too much to feel, and hence the mind dissociates from the body.

The mildest form of dissociation is a subtle leaving of your body, which means you are not aware of your body. The most severe version would be a complete dissociative episode or even psychosis.

Dr. Levine describes dissociation:

It protects us from being overwhelmed by escalating arousal, fear, and pain. It "softens" the pain of severe injury by secreting nature's internal opium, the endorphins. In trauma, dissociation seems to be a favored means of enabling a person to endure experiences that are, at the moment, beyond endurance.

**From *Healing Trauma: A Pioneering Program
for Restoring the Wisdom of Your Body*[6]**

Some of the symptoms of trauma can be easily detected:

- **A frozen gaze and/or lack of blinking**
  This is a common sign, both in acute and old trauma. You will see someone just not blink, as if the second they blink, something horrible could happen.

- **Tingling in hands or feet**
  This often combines with feeling light-headed or slightly numb and generally disconnected.

- **Prone to injury**
  Another telltale sign is frequent bumping into the corners of cupboards and furniture or becoming very clumsy and dropping items.

- **Unresponsive to questions or instructions**
  The internal disconnection results in an inability to connect with others as well. This often results in diminished agency, meaning you are not entirely able to make decisions and set boundaries.

In this book, we are looking at trauma mostly for the sake of understanding one of the most common bodily responses in women, which is the "freeze" response. In addition to fight and flight, there is a third trauma response, which is freeze. Freeze is an interesting phenomenon, because freeze essentially stops us in our tracks and makes us hunker down. This can be physical inertia or a mental and emotional lockdown. Understanding, detecting, and undoing freeze is one of the biggest contributors to a fully embodied, alive, and pleasurable life.

....

Understanding, detecting, and undoing freeze is one of the biggest
contributors to a fully embodied, alive, and pleasurable life.

....

Freeze is said to be more common in women. There is some emerging research that says this has to do with the necessity for women in ancient times to stay very quiet and hidden with the children when fighting was not possible, or to hide from a predator.

What makes freeze hard to detect is that, in this state, we don't know that something is not right. Because we are frozen, we are disconnected from sensations and think that we feel fine. Even our body feels very calm. People may look from the outside and remark how serene we are. The vagus nerve, which is involved in the freeze mechanism, actually slows down the heart rate, contrary to what happens in the flight response, which results in a speeding up. If your freeze comes with immobility, it is easier to detect:

- Lack of blinking/fixed gaze
- Flat affect, meaning not much emotion is shown on the face
- Physical immobility
- Slower than usual movement and sluggishness
- Mental and emotional fixedness: slow responses and answers

Freeze can happen after fresh trauma or can be triggered by old trauma; either way, it will result in an inability to feel and connect. All trauma responses leave us disconnected from our biggest ally, the body. Through the body, trauma can be unraveled, and the body's natural intelligence can release trauma much better than our mind does.

> All trauma responses leave us disconnected from our
> biggest ally, the body. Through the body, trauma can
> be unraveled, and the body's natural intelligence can
> release trauma much better than our mind does.

When trauma has been triggered in our body, there are several possible actions we can take; first and foremost is to always come back to the body. Here are some simple steps:

- Blink, then blink again, and again. In my experience this is by far the most effective action.
- Move your hands, move your feet, wiggle your toes.
- Look down at your feet, feel the ground underneath you.
- Orient yourself in your surroundings. Look at the floor, look out windows, determine what day and time it is in your mind.

Initially, all that might be possible is a blink or the wiggling of a finger, but that movement will often set in motion the body's natural response to trauma.

The key is to keep moving until feeling returns to the body. In my years of working with clients, I have developed a somatic release method called The Non-Linear Movement Method®, which is specifically designed to unblock freeze and release trauma from the body. You will find detailed instructions in section IV: "Sacred Practices of the Wild Woman," pp. 197–236.

Often when people are involved in a traumatic event and are taken to a safe place or hospital, they are completely frozen. Sometimes a hug or some movement will unravel everything and they will start to shake and cry, which is the body's natural response. This will allow the body to release. The worst you can do for someone—or yourself—in that situation is to hold and soothe them (or yourself) in order try to stop this natural process.

Finally, another aspect of freeze worth mentioning is that it sometimes happens in sexual occasions. It could be that old events and memories get triggered, some of which you might not even remember or think of as traumatic. Or the pleasure is so intense that freeze sets in. Either way, for the sexual occasion, the same principles apply. Stop, and then move your body in ways that bring you back to what you are feeling. Only then should you decide what you would like to happen next.

Obviously, if you are dealing with more extreme trauma and injuries, please see a qualified professional. This chapter is meant to give you a general understanding of what hinders embodiment and some tools for mild cases of disembodiment and freeze.

8

Intuition

I WOKE UP WITH A START AND A GASP AT 4:00 A.M. COMING OUT OF A deep sleep, I knew there was something horribly wrong. The words coming out of my mouth as I crawled out of bed, still disoriented, were "I lost James."

James was my coteacher, close friend, and collaborator in all things creative. We taught workshops together and he had recently moved from Victoria, Canada, to Santa Monica, California. We had rented a huge loft close to the beach where he lived and where we both taught regularly. We had just received funding for a big online interactive learning platform and recently returned from our first European teaching trip.

James and I were very close. We had known each other for five years and worked together for four. We shared several obscure interests and delighted in creating fun outings and events together. Aside from my husband, James was the person I enjoyed being with the most.

Exactly a year earlier, to the day, James's father had died from organ failure related to Crohn's disease. It had taken a long, agonizing week in the hospital. At the time, James was still a registered nurse (even though he had changed careers quite a few years back) and he took care of his father until the very end. This had had an enormous impact on James, and he had gone to the desert to spend a few days alone, to connect with his memories and the anniversary of his father's death.

We had a brief phone call before he left in which he told me that he had packed mementos and a picture of his father, as well as food, drinks, and supplies for camping out. He was an experienced outdoorsman, loved the desert, and was also a trained lifeguard and paramedic. He traveled in his beloved camper van, which was kitted out for his visits to Burning Man and his Zen teacher's desert retreat. Before ending our call, he told me he would be back Tuesday morning before our regular Tuesday night class.

There was absolutely no reason for my sudden feeling of panic in the middle of the night. I went to the kitchen and drank some water, trying to calm myself down. My body ached, and I had a strange pain in my chest and sternum. I walked around for a bit, trying to shake what I thought were the remnants of a nightmare. Eventually I went to the spare bedroom, so as not to disturb my husband. There, I spent the last few hours of the night in a mixture of panic and pain, with an odd feeling of disconnection from my body. I wondered what was going on with James, but figured that since it was the night of his father's death, he was conducting a ritual of some sort and allowing himself to grieve, and that I was just picking something up in the midst of a nightmare.

When it was finally time to get up, I was relieved the night was over and packed up to drive to Los Angeles to see clients during the day and teach with James at night. I expected to get a message from James as soon as he was back in cell phone range, but I did not hear from him. By the time I got in my car to drive to the loft, I was seriously worried but still telling myself that he had probably come back tired and had a nap. At the loft, his car was nowhere to be seen, and the place was not prepared for the fifty people arriving in less than an hour.

I knew then that whatever I had experienced the night before was exactly what it had felt like, despite my denial that something was seriously wrong. There was absolutely no way that he would not be back for any reason other than that he was not able to come back.

Meanwhile, people were arriving, and we had a sold-out event that night. I had no evidence that what I had felt was real, and I did not want to falsely alarm anyone. I told our assistants that James had been held up and proceeded to teach a three-hour class by myself that night. On every break, I would run to the green room to throw up and make frantic phone calls to anyone I thought might know where he could have gone.

James was intensely private and kept his plans and whereabouts secret, even from me. All I knew was that he was "in the desert," which in Southern California means at least five possible places, all spread far apart from one another. When the event was finished and everyone had left, it was past 11:00 p.m. and I was out of options. Part of me was sure he had died, while another part was hoping he was just stuck somewhere and I could find him. I went to the police department not far from the loft to report him missing and was told I needed to report him missing wherever he had gone missing . . . Right!

I finally gathered myself and sat down. I had learned all kinds of practices of "feeling out" from my teacher over the years. She would take me to the pond and teach me how to feel into the water and detect the fish. She taught me how to walk through the forest silently and feel out in all directions, locating animals and finding objects.

"Feeling out" is an integral part of Deity Yoga instruction, where it is used to visualize the surroundings of the archetype we work with. But my teacher wanted my skills also to be useful in real life, so she taught me how to connect with nature, animals, and people that way. It is a simple process of quieting the mind, relaxing the body, and then spreading the quiet awareness out from one's body. (I will give you more detailed instructions on this practice on p. 111, "Feeling Out," at the end of this chapter.)

I quieted my mind—not easy in the midst of all of this—and started to "feel out," connecting with James from my body to his body, and suddenly, I had a distinct image and a direction. I jumped into the car, determined to find him, and started driving the two and a half hours toward Joshua Tree. I had seen an image of large round boulders piled in a specific formation and remembered some pictures James had shown me of his favorite spot in Joshua Tree, which matched the picture in my mind's eye.

I was driving and "feeling out," "feeling out" and driving, mumbling prayers and making bargains with God under my breath all the while. I called the park rangers, who were polite but not very helpful. I would have to wait until the office opened in the morning. So I took myself straight to the Joshua Tree police station, still dressed in my workshop gear. I had not slept, eaten, or even had a drink of water since the workshop had ended.

The closer I came to Joshua Tree, the more certain I was that that was where James was. I sat in the park entrance lot, my senses spreading out, trying to locate him. Once again, I had a clear image, this time with a large rock on the right and a juniper bush on the left. Where to start? The park was huge, and I did not know my way around. I was still wearing my flimsy sandals from the night before, and was told by the rangers that I should not look for James because, if he was lost, they would need clear footprints leading from his car in order to begin a search, and my walking around could potentially disturb them.

Filing a missing-person report is not for the faint of heart. Having had no contact with American law enforcement beforehand, I was absolutely unprepared for the experience. At some point I was asked to give my fingerprints, and my driver's license was taken from me. I just wanted to go look for him, but I was not allowed to leave for quite a while. All the information I gave them about him seemed to be less important than who I was and where I had been while he disappeared.

I felt like I was losing my mind, stuck at the police station with an uncompassionate officer, and still with nothing to eat or drink. The long wait at the station was interrupted only by a few anguishing phone calls with James's sister and his mother. Imagine having to tell a mother on the first anniversary of her husband's death that her only son had gone missing.

Later that afternoon, after I had checked on every John Doe in the state of California and had gone through the reports of all unidentified patients in hospitals—I was still going only on my intuition that he actually was where I had reported him missing—the park rangers found his car in one of the campgrounds. I was relieved to have been correct.

Much happened in the next days that is not relevant to this part of the story, but I will forever remember the mixture of hope and knowing deep down that he was gone, feeling myself suspended in a strange limbo. Then, at 2:00 the next morning, I was awoken by the coroner calling me in my cheap desert motel room. They had found James and, as I had known in my body, he had been dead for a while.

When I was finally allowed to see where they had found him, my internal navigation knew exactly where to go. It felt like I was following a thread to where he had died, lying between a large boulder on his right and a juniper bush on his left, exactly as I had seen it in my mind's eye. It turned out that he had accidentally slid down a steep slope and hit the rock chest first, causing internal injuries. In his last moments, he had propped himself against the rock, turned his gaze up to the sky, and passed on.

There is no way to adequately describe the anguish of losing someone deeply loved. No way to express what it felt like to give his family the news. No way to detail the many steps it took to find out what had happened, to identify him, claim his belongings and his van, pack up his things—the clothes were the worst, each holding a memory and his scent—and pick out the garments for him to be cremated in.

Then finally, almost three weeks later, on a hot, late June morning, I left my house in James's van, with his belongings in the back, and drove the three hours south to Indio to collect his ashes. I had promised his family not to let his remains out of my sight, so I packed the box that held his ashes into a pretty carrier bag and set them next to me between the seats of the van. From my seat, I could see his name printed on the outside.

And then James and I went on a final three-day road trip, all the way from Indio, California, to Victoria, British Columbia. The journey deserves a whole book in itself, but needless to say it was at times unbearable, at times heart-opening in the most profound way, and at times laugh-out-loud comical. I shared the second day of driving with James's closest friend, Kevin, and we talked and cried the whole time. I stayed at a wonderful friend's farm in Oregon the second night and slept hugging the box of ashes. I took him with me wherever I went: ladies' rooms, for a drink in a brewery with Kevin, on the deck of the ferry to Victoria. The most difficult moment of the journey came when I handed the box of ashes to his mother and his sisters. The loss I felt in that moment is still indescribable.

This whole experience changed my life profoundly. Much of what had contributed to James's accidental death, the confluences of dates and events, the people I encountered along the way, is too strange to recall without much more space than this chapter allows. All of it has shaped me into the woman I am today, and much of it informs how I live my life, how I teach, and how I love.

One of the many realizations that followed these events was that my intuition had been so accurate. I had nothing else to fall back on, so I had followed my internal navigation with much less doubt than I would normally have done.

All of it felt very surreal to me, and it took quite a while to process that I had woken up that early morning and felt him dying, that my body pains had correlated to his injuries, that I had followed my intuition to where he was lost and helped find him. The accuracy of my visuals was startling, even to me, someone who is used to "seeing things." (I have a photographic memory, so I am used to processing visually.)

Am I "clairvoyant," an "intuitive," a "remote viewer"? I would certainly not say so. Those are labels used to make sense of and give importance to the most ancient of natural skills.

Intuition and clear perception are skills that are part of our human heritage. We survived and thrived as a species because we could sense and feel far beyond what our minds could cognitively process. Nonverbal communication, feeling and connecting with others, and sensing danger are all the most essential aspects of staying connected and alive as a tribe.

> Intuition and clear perception are skills that are part of our human heritage. We survived and thrived as a species because we could sense and feel far beyond what our minds could cognitively process.

As women, we have strong perceptive abilities: they're part of staying connected to our babies and children. Most mothers have experienced this bond, with some reporting that they can be out shopping and suddenly sense that their baby is hungry, and feel their milk come in right before getting a phone call from home confirming this perception. Intuition has long been made the domain of women because of our heightened awareness of surroundings and our connection to others, which was once, and still is, necessary to keep our children alive.

However, men are equipped with equally fine feeling ability and have used it for hunting, protection from enemies, and guarding livestock. In ancient times, both men and women acted as seers, oracles, and shamans.

> In ancient times, both men and women acted as seers, oracles, and shamans.

We all have the ability to feel, sense, and intuit. Just how much we do these things depends mostly on two factors: perceptivity and skill training. These two, combined, determine how much we are able to intuit and perceive. We can train ourselves in both aspects. As with any skill, different people will have different talents. This is very much like learning an instrument. Everyone can do it, but some people will be extraordinarily gifted musicians while others might not have a lot of natural talent and need to work harder at mastery.

Perceptivity

How much we can perceive depends to a large degree on how relaxed our body is. As with pleasure, how much we are embodied and sensitized determines how fully we can perceive. The information is always available, but the stimuli of modern life can both acutely and habitually dull our sensory perception. The noise and tension of a stressful life can drown out the intuitive information our body continuously receives.

To train perception, all the sensitizing and embodiment practices found in the "Sacred Practices of the Wild Woman" section apply (section IV, pp. 197–236). By learning how to relax and listen to the signals of your body, you will be able to deepen your intuitive ability considerably.

Skill Development

Much of intuitive skill is not magic but a matter of making distinctions. The more distinctions you can make, the finer your perception. It is very much like wine tasting or distinguishing smells for perfumery, in that it is something that can be learned. If you know nothing about wine and someone gives you a taste, all you can determine is whether or not you enjoy the wine. However, once someone knowledgeable gives you instruction as to what to look for, you can acquire the ability to make distinctions.

Much of intuitive skill is not magic, but a matter
of making distinctions. The more distinctions
you can make, the finer your perception.

In wine tasting, someone would ask you what you can smell—is it fruity, flowery, or resinous? They'll ask what tastes you can perceive as the wine rolls over your tongue. Can you taste whether the wine is heavy or light? Over time, you accumulate information about those tastes and smells that then translates into being able to recognize what kind of wine you are drinking. To the untrained person, it appears to be a superhuman feat when someone can take a sip and declare, "This is a Chateau Margaux."

Training your intuition works in very much the same way. You can learn to distinguish different signs and signals. For instance, if you want to train yourself to be able to tell if someone is lying, the first thing to do is find a situation in which someone has lied to you. Remember how you felt while it happened. Mostly people will say in hindsight something like, "I knew something was wrong!"

Remember where in the body you felt the "wrong." Describe to yourself the texture, temperature, and feeling of that area in your body. The more detailed you can be, the better. Once you know the feeling, you can train yourself to pay attention when it "lights up" in your body. Each time it does, check on how accurate you were and fine-tune your perception. Over time, your body will be able to send you distinct signals for distinct incidents.

Here is an example: You are sitting with a good friend and you ask her what she did during the weekend. She answers you by listing a few activities and then casually moves on to another topic. You have a funny feeling about the way she answered you; something does not feel right. There is a bit of tension in your solar plexus, a slight feeling of unease, but she has moved on in the conversation, and you push the feeling aside. Later on, you find out that she went on a date with an ex-boyfriend of yours. This is usually the moment we say, "I knew it!"

If you want to train your perception, you'll let yourself go back to the conversation in your mind. Remember as many details as you can, both what was said and what you perceived in her body. Try to recall the feeling of unease you had and notice the exact texture and location in your body. In this instance, it was a dull, achy sensation right over your diaphragm. Then, next time you notice that sensation in your body, you can be alert already. Track the sensation and what it is connected to. Over time, you will be able to link certain bodily sensations with specific external events—in this case, someone lying to you.

As you train yourself to become aware in this way, you will be able to distinguish many different layers of information through your body.

The same applies to visual and auditory clues. For instance, when I used to see eight clients a day, I sat across from people, observing and listening to them all day long. I became aware of every little shift, every micro-expression, the subtle flush of skin, the change in breathing and, over time, even the changes in smell. I had many years to learn those fine distinctions, and by now those distinctions are all part of my internal data—so much so that I no longer need to analyze them; the information just rises into my conscious mind.

Notice that I used my work environment to train my perception. Your day-to-day life, with all its difficulties and inconveniences, holds many untapped opportunities for this kind of training. What are you exposed to in your life that you can bring more attention to? How can you use your daily routine and circumstances to hone your awareness and sensitivity? Training your perception takes time and repetition. Finding day-to-day scenarios, for instance with coworkers, will give you adequate opportunity to hone your skills.

Different people process information differently. Some are more visual, others auditory, and still others are primarily guided by feeling. You might receive intuitive information through thoughts forming in your mind, or by internally "hearing" sentences, or, as in my case, by seeing visual information. It doesn't matter which way you perceive, the important thing is that you get to know your own way of processing the world and that you can link the information with the accompanying physical sensations. That way, you can simply rely on your body sending the message and interpret the sensation through previous experience.

> Different people process information differently.
> Some are more visual, others auditory, and still
> others are primarily guided by feeling.

Ever since I was very young, I have loved animals and spent much of my time observing and connecting with them. I would sneak off to a nearby pond—my parents did not want me to go there, as I could not swim yet—and sit perfectly still until the frogs and toads, and the snakes that hunted them, would all come out. I spent hours watching, deeply immersed, and would often completely forget everything else. I learned their behaviors and became aware of the different sounds they made. Over time, I could sense the frogs before they appeared and feel the snakes in the grass without seeing them. My body became finely attuned to their bodies, so much so that, even today, I can sense animals anywhere.

My very first teacher, who instructed me in herb lore, could feel where in the woods herbs and mushrooms grew. She could stalk chanterelles like a hunter stalks deer. She explained to me that she learned to do so the same way I had learned about the frogs. She would get to know the woods, sit for long periods of time and observe the movement of the sun, where the dew would gather and where certain plants grew. She had done so for close to forty years when I met her and could predict where the best mushrooms would grow long before the season started.

Training and cultivating your intuition allows for a more holistic decision-making process. The stronger and clearer our intuition, the better it can be factored into choices and opportunities.

Training and cultivating your intuition allows for a more holistic decision-making process. The stronger and clearer our intuition, the better it can be factored into choices and opportunities.

A friend of mine had a choice between two very exciting job offers. She spent some time analyzing the apparent aspects such as pay, benefits, opportunities for growth within the company, and job responsibilities. Once she had ascertained the viability of both offers, she sat for a while and imagined herself in each position. She allowed her body to feel and relaxed her thoughts. After a short while, she felt a very strong intuition to take one of the offers over the other. She followed that feeling, knowing that she had already given it enough thought with her rational mind. It turned out to be exactly the right decision; about six months later, the other company she had not chosen encountered a problem with their IPO offering and laid off all new hires.

You can also learn to use your intuition to feel out people and circumstances the way I did as part of my lineage training; the same principles apply. First, observe and collect data; then integrate the data by checking the accuracy of your observation, using hindsight to check if your feelings were right or wrong. Learn which part of your body "lights up" and how to notice that, then fine-tune with more observation. After a while this all becomes second nature, and the intuitive information flows more freely.

The key with all this learning is to stay away from processing or questioning the information cognitively. Once that happens, the raw data sent from your body becomes tainted by doubt, projection, and mental chatter. Our agendas and conditionings can get in the way of the intuitive process.

Once you have acquired data and can accurately listen to the messages of your body, you can also train to "feel out."

Feeling Out

To "feel out," you begin by relaxing the body. You can lie down or sit in a stable, relaxed position and close your eyes. Then scan your body, relaxing one area after the other from the top of the head to the bottom of the feet. Next, allow your mind to settle. The key here is not to force the mind into stillness by applying a technique like counting or focusing on breath, but rather let the thoughts and mental loops gradually unwind in their own time. This might take a while at first if you are not used to sitting in stillness. Once your body feels relaxed and your mind has unwound, you can start the process of "feeling out." Begin by feeling your body and where it meets the floor or surface you touch. Then feel your position in the room. It might take some time to learn how to feel these things without getting distracted. Over time, you will get better at keeping your attention stable and you can spread your awareness out, first through the entire room, to all its corners, then beyond the room, and so on. This way you can train yourself to spread your awareness up into the sky by feeling a bit farther upward each time, all the way into outer space, and down into the ground, all the way to the earth's core. Eventually, you will be able to "feel out" to someone specific, as I did with James.

These days, five years after James's accidental death, I rarely doubt my intuition. The whole experience has changed who I am on many levels, and has definitely taught me that I can trust what I feel. When I see clients, consult with companies, or teach students, I allow my intuition to be part of my work, with the intention of bringing all my skills to the table for the benefit of everyone I meet.

9

Pleasure Is Our Birthright

A SUCCESSFUL AND DRIVEN DERMATOLOGIST, WITH A CLINIC SPECIALIZING in cosmetic treatments and skin rejuvenations, Tina looked the picture of a well-put-together, fit, and prosperous career woman. At one of my Wild Woman's Way trainings, she raised her hand during a Q&A. She told the women present that she had studied hard all through her medical training and that her goal had been to create a clinic that would allow her to be financially independent quickly, a goal she had long since achieved. She met her husband, an artist and woodworker, at a friend's art opening, and they married and had a baby right after she finished her residency.

Now, five years later, with the help of vigorous workouts, she had regained her body; the baby had grown into a toddler; her clinic no longer needed her attention full time; and she finally had some space to look at her life. Sadly, she did not like what she saw. Even though she had reached all her goals, she felt unsatisfied in her relationship and disconnected from herself.

To support her and the baby, her husband had taken on the role of stay-at-home father, tending to their son and creating art in his backyard studio. He provided healthy meals for his family, managed the bills and household, and created fun family outings on weekends. Nevertheless, despite his best efforts, Tina was resentful toward him.

She felt the burden of being the provider and at the same time could not let go of controlling every aspect of her life. Her husband's way of handling things felt "too slow" or "not right" for her, and she would often take over just to "get things done." Even when she wanted to let go of control, her body was on high alert, and her mind would habitually go into planning mode. She told us that she just could not let go, even on her days off; and she did not feel like connecting sexually with her husband, or with herself, at all.

Even though she had enjoyed sex when she and her husband had first met, there had always been other, more important issues: the pressure of exams, residency, setting up a business, and then pregnancy and the baby.

When she decided to connect with her sexuality and started reading books and articles about it, she began to feel like she was stunted, and had missed out on a whole aspect of her life. To compensate, she decided to apply the same performance expectations and rigor to her sexuality that she had to her career and body, but the more techniques she tried, the less her body responded.

Her husband, supportive as always, wanted to connect sexually and even learned how to give her massages, but no matter what he did or she attempted, her mind would get in the way, her body could not relax, and her frustration grew.

She told us that she came to our workshops in the hope that she could figure out a way to connect her mind and her body and become a sexually alive woman. She had recently considered having an affair with a man whom she thought could open her body. The fact that she was even considering such an extreme solution worried her and drove her to finally reach out to ask for help.

Tina was suffering from what I call "Superwoman Syndrome." Highly accomplished, smart, and driven, she is a dedicated, loving mother and a career woman. She manages to care for herself and her body while maintaining a relationship and social life. For her, and for many women living different variations of this story, the high standards and discipline they apply to their lives do not translate well to pleasure and sexuality.

Tina began to understand that pushing herself toward achieving pleasure was creating tension and numbness, which were counteractive to what she wanted to achieve. Instead, she began to practice relaxing and listening to her body, which helped her to access her natural sensuality.

Once she became empowered in her own sexuality, her relationship with her husband gradually improved and deepened. By being able to supply her own pleasure, she no longer expected her husband to be responsible. This took the pressure off their intimacy, and her newfound sensuality allowed them to connect more deeply and enjoy being with each other without the stress of performance anxiety.

Nowadays, Tina is hardly recognizable. Glowing, relaxed, and easygoing, she is a far cry from the tight, controlled, and unhappy woman who raised her hand at that workshop. She is now introducing embodiment and relaxation practices to the women who come to her clinic for beauty treatments.

The Superwoman Syndrome

Tina, like many other students and clients I have worked with over the years, grew up with divergent cultural messages and a plethora of media images that influenced the way she perceived herself. On one hand, we are still expected to adhere to moral standards of being a "good girl" and not engage in too much casual sex; on the other hand, we see pop-culture icons celebrated for acting and dressing like porn stars. We are told that career and independence are of utmost importance, but at the same time, beauty and youth are celebrated as the ultimate achievement.

> We are told that career and independence are of utmost importance, but at the same time, beauty and youth are celebrated as the ultimate achievement.

We have been led to believe that we can be everything in all domains. The messages are now coming not only from women's magazines and social media but also from successful women themselves.

High-performance businesswomen have written books about climbing the corporate ladder while sharing parenting responsibilities with their equally successful partners. The message given is that we can advance our careers and should not be held back by our wish to have children or a partnership, and that with discipline and a strategy of not being "nice," we can accomplish everything a man can and still put our children to bed at the end of the workday.

Social media accounts portray the perfect lifestyle. A quick scroll through Instagram will provide a revealing snapshot of our current cultural climate. We can find something for every one of our dreams, aspirations, and insecurities: there are the perfectly styled women with beautiful, well-behaved children in perfectly decorated houses; the scantily dressed yoga teachers posing in pretzel-like postures on beautiful beaches; goddesses in flowing gauzy garbs dancing around a fire; globe-trotting "digital nomad" internet entrepreneurs who claim to work four hours a week; and famous internet pleasure coaches demonstrating their sexual fitness by weightlifting surfboards with their vaginas.

The list of aspirational materials is endless, with much emphasis placed on being beautiful, fit, and sexually desirable, as well as on having purpose and a career.

No wonder we place incredibly high standards on ourselves, our lives, and our sexual experiences.

These multiple demands are nothing new. Jerry Hall, supermodel and mother of four children with her former rock-star partner Mick Jagger, famously quoted her mother's advice to her as a teenager: "To keep a man you must be a maid in the living room, a cook in the kitchen and a whore in the bedroom." Today, we could add "CEO/entrepreneur in the boardroom."

Many women I have worked with juggle the various aspects of their lives with great resourcefulness and joy, yet find it increasingly difficult to experience pleasure, or to find or maintain a healthy relationship.

Not many areas of our lives are as fraught with conflict and controversy as women's pleasure and sexuality, and its expression.

The age-old "Madonna/whore complex" is still at play in our minds, competing with newer tropes of modern icons like Kim Kardashian, who came to fame with a sex tape, but then used sex and her looks to create vast business success, a high-profile marriage, and status.

On one hand, we are supposed to be empowered in our sexual expression, while on the other, there are still the persistent messages that owning one's pleasure is frivolous and makes us "sluts," and that men have sex with "those" kinds of women—the whores—but want to marry "decent" women—the Madonnas—i.e., capable, dependable mothers who are also competent, even-keeled businesswomen, and who somehow should turn into wild creatures in the bedroom—but only with the right, respectable partner, of course.

There is also the persistent message from the evolutionary psychology camp that men are irresistibly attracted only to young, radiant, fertile women. To make matters worse, with the widespread use of internet porn, men, and increasingly more women, have a distorted view of what sex looks and sounds like.

As we internalize these divergent messages and impossibly high standards of physical fitness, beauty, and sexual expression, we fall prey to the Superwoman Syndrome. Increasingly alienated from our bodies' natural perception and ways of unfolding, we apply tricks, hacks, and techniques to try to force our way into feeling turned on, sexy, and radiant. And somewhere along the way, we lose track of who we really are.

> Increasingly alienated from our bodies' natural perception and ways of unfolding, we apply tricks, hacks, and techniques to try to force our way into feeling turned on, sexy, and radiant. And somewhere along the way, we lose track of who we really are.

Turning our attention back to Tina: what she eventually came to realize was that she could not make her body respond by applying pressure and expectation. We can't force "being" by "doing." The first step to claiming sensual and sexual aliveness is relaxation.

Once the body learns to relax habitual tension and clench, we can begin to sensitize and regain a connection to our feeling body. We can perceive life, our emotions, and our bodies as they are and find pleasure in the sensory perceptions that are already available.

> Once the body learns to relax habitual tension and clench, we can begin to sensitize and regain a connection to our feeling body.

This sensual awareness directly contributes to our sexual aliveness and responsiveness. Because our body is already sensually awake, sexual pleasure does not have to build from 0 (equaling total numbness) to 100 (equaling orgasm). Instead, we can enjoy the sensual engagement with everyday life and keep ourselves at a relaxed 70, which makes bridging the gap toward orgasm so much more possible.

When we come back to our very own feeling body, we realize that,

as women, we are built for a life of sensual engagement. When we come
back to utilizing our five senses, we inevitably experience a richness and
sensual awareness that encompass every aspect of our lives, including
our very own expression of sexuality.

Our bodies are miraculous, fertile grounds of creation and creativity. Every month of our fertile years we travel the roller coaster of misery
and ecstasy, moments of high and low sensitivity to both pleasure and
pain, and peaks and valleys of desire.

. . . .

**Our bodies are miraculous, fertile grounds of creation and
creativity. Every month of our fertile years we travel the roller
coaster of misery and ecstasy, moments of high and low sensitivity
to both pleasure and pain, and peaks and valleys of desire.**

. . . .

In our menopausal years and beyond, we add experience and a certain surrender to life into the mix, which, as many women report, can
add a whole new layer of aliveness, richness, and freedom to our sensual
experience.

Pleasure is deeply individual, depending on many factors, some biological and anatomical, some emotional. There is always a wild card of
magic and mystery involved. Sometimes pleasure eludes us and other
times it is so heightened we can barely contain it.

However, there are building blocks to sensual and sexual aliveness,
which are detailed here below.

We are mostly focusing on the underlying principles and wider considerations around pleasure here, with practices that enable and empower you to form your own relationship and experience with your
pleasure body. Instead of telling you what you "should" experience, the
following steps are meant to educate you and facilitate inquiry into your
body's responses, so that you become empowered in your relationship
with sensual and sexual living.

Some women get confused and even ashamed when I discuss pleasure exercises, since, for many of us, pleasure is connected only to sex. We can feel shy about experiencing pleasure in our bodies, but the truth is that pleasure is much bigger than just sex: experience the feeling of clothing on your skin, the enjoyment of a delicious piece of chocolate on your tongue, or the wonderful sensations of stroking the fur of a beloved pet.

....

We can feel shy about experiencing pleasure in our bodies,
but the truth is that pleasure is much bigger than just sex:
experience the feeling of clothing on your skin, the enjoyment
of a delicious piece of chocolate on your tongue, or the
wonderful sensations of stroking the fur of a beloved pet.

....

When you discover that practicing relaxation, engagement with your five senses, and sensitizing your body is how pleasure starts, you'll develop a much broader view of sensuality and your body.

Here are the different aspects that, when combined, lead to a fully empowered sensual and sexual life. These concepts and exercises focus on self-practice first. Regardless of whether you have a partner or not, being intimately familiar with your own body, and its patterns of sensual awareness and sexual aliveness, is the ultimate empowerment.

We will look at these different building blocks separately, even though they are all present anytime we experience the fullness of sensation, which we can finally reclaim as our birthright.

Relaxation

Like Tina, many of us spend most of our days in our head. We think, direct, and plan. We sit, type, and drive. Our minds stay active long after the heady work is done.

There are many reasons why a woman can't or might not want to relax, some of which need to be addressed by a qualified counselor. But, as a rule, by attending to the body, we can return to feeling and relaxation.

Even if our mental stress is justified, by bringing our attention and energy back into the body, our mental chatter and emotional tension often subside. Bringing the energy into the lower body relieves the tension, clench, and tightness in the head, jaw, and shoulders.

One of the prevalent curses of the modern woman is tension in the lower body and pelvic floor. Along with sitting for long periods of time, and experiencing chronic stress and overwhelm, we have to contend with cultural conditionings around not breathing into the belly, lest we look fat. This leads to lack of embodiment and leaves the lower body numb.

Most women tend to have a tight pelvic floor, a slightly clenched anus and buttocks, and a tight belly. On a physical level, this impedes blood flow and suppresses arousal. On an energetic level, these and related areas of our bodies that open and relax for pleasure are habitually tight and hence less accessible.

Over the past twenty years, I have found that most women have a chronically tight, pulled-up pelvic floor and that, for many of them, Kegel exercises are actually useless, since the weakness in the pelvic floor comes from muscle fatigue and not from loose, overly relaxed muscles. Often women with chronic tension do better by learning to relax the lower body and strengthening another layer of the pelvic floor by doing squats instead of Kegels.

For a richer sexual experience, relaxation of the body and mind are key. (You'll find additional practices for calming the mind and opening the body in section IV: "Sacred Practices of the Wild Woman," pp. 197–236.)

With clitoral orgasms, we tend to tense our bodies in order to achieve climax, but afterward, our bodies relax, and women often experience an emotional release. For G-spot and cervical orgasms, as well as for whole-body pleasure, relaxation of the lower body and particularly the core are key.

The core consists of the muscles of your torso that keep you supported, including your abdominals and back muscles. When these muscles are habitually tense, less feeling and sensation is available.

Here is a simple practice you can do to explore those areas and subtly relax for deeper pleasure:

Relaxation for Pleasure

Lying in a comfortable position on the floor or bed, turn your attention to your lower body. Put a hand on your belly, below the belly button. Allow your breath to flow into your lungs deeply but without pushing. Notice how your belly moves up and down with each breath. Let your breath flow naturally, without influencing rhythm or depth, and relax your body a bit more with each breath, passively dissolving tension in your belly and lower body. Sense whether you can unclench your buttocks, relax your thighs, and your pelvic girdle and floor. Most important is that you become aware of tension and clench, not that it all dissolves. What is much of habitual tension will take a while to do so; by identifying the areas of tension in this practice, you can, every so often throughout your day, bring your attention to your lower body and unclench when you notice tension arising.

Sensual Pleasure

See. Hear. Touch. Smell. Taste. These are the five simple ingredients for a sensual, pleasurable life.

We engage with the world through our senses, but often in modern life our bodies respond with irritation or numbness to the overwhelming sensory input to which we are exposed.

"See" registers to our nervous system as clutter or excessive computer in-flow; "hear" flinches at loud traffic noise; "touch" becomes irritation, as people bump against us in the subway; "smell" reacts to exhaust fumes and perfumes; and "taste" tolerates quick convenience foods.

When the stimuli are consistently too high, our body will try to narrow our sensory perception. Eventually, our nervous system will numb to sensations and only the "loudest" will register at all.

Lowering sensory aggravation is one obvious strategy to feeling more. Developing a stronger nervous system is another. There are practices for both, to help us feel more in the moment, and to gradually make a lifestyle change, which you can find in section IV: "Sacred Practices of the Wild Woman," pp. 197–236. However, sometimes life circumstances just aren't conducive to quiet, and not everyone can relocate to the serene countryside or a Himalayan cave.

There is a sensual pleasure to feeling one's body and engaging in activities that awaken the senses, and it is always available to us. We can use everyday life to sensually enliven us and bring us back to feeling and our bodies.

By bringing active and conscious attention to our five senses throughout the day, we train our body to become sensually enlivened, and we redirect our sensitivity toward pleasure.

See

Wherever you are, find things of beauty and joy to look at. If you spend consistent time in one place, such as your office or a place in your house, you can create specific displays that give you pleasure when you look at them. (See section IV: "Sacred Practices of the Wild Woman," pp. 197–236.) Or you can seek out and focus on anything in your visual field that creates a positive sensation in your body. The key is to focus on something you enjoy rather than something that disturbs your nervous system.

Hear

Get yourself a pair of noise-canceling headphones and listen to recorded sounds of nature or music you enjoy on the train, in the gym, or anywhere else you find appropriate. Make playlists that you choose to give you sensual pleasure. If you can, find a quiet place to sit and enjoy the peace and give your hearing a break. Or, if you can go into nature, focus on the rustling of wind in the trees, birds singing, or the sound of a stream or ocean. Focus on the different sounds and then let them melt together and become like a gentle massage.

Touch

Feel your world through your hands. Touch the different textures of your surroundings consciously and notice what sensations they produce. Notice what happens when you wrap your hands around a warm teacup or a glass of ice water. Carry a small, smooth stone or ridged shell you can touch in your pocket. Caress the fur of an animal and the soft hair of your child, and delight in the sensations.

Smell

Before you take a bite of your food or a sip of your drink, inhale its scent. As you inhale, imagine the scent moving into your body. Let the smell register, and notice how your body reacts. Wait until you can feel your body's reaction before you eat or drink.

Taste

After you have thoroughly enjoyed its scent, take a bite of your food and taste it deliberately. Notice where in your body the taste registers, and any emotions you might feel. Eating is a deeply sensual and emotional act, and the more you are smelling and tasting, the better your relationship with your food and your body will be.

Take a moment to define pleasurable activities for each sense for yourself and begin incorporating sensory enjoyment and awareness into your life. You'll notice gradual, subtle shifts in your body and energy levels as you engage all your senses consciously.

This present-moment awareness will translate into the sexual domain, since your sensory system will already be trained to be alive and sensitive. All the practices described in section IV: "Sacred Practices of the Wild Woman," pp. 197–236, are conducive to sensual development.

Sensitization

Heightened sensual awareness results in heightened sexual experience and receptivity. A sensitized, relaxed, and sensually awake body is more ready and able to engage sexually.

For my workshops, I have developed a specific practice, which I call the "Background Pleasure Practice," described below. I use this for myself and for the women I teach as a bridge between sensual engagement and sexual arousal.

One of the main obstacles to sexual desire and arousal is the vast distance between the in-your-head, disembodied state that comes with living a busy life and the toe-curling orgasms we desire. Many women I have worked with say that it feels like too much to confront that gap, and that trying to do so often feels like yet another chore after a full day. So they would rather sit on the sofa and watch TV, or even work a bit more, than follow the long path from numbness to pleasure. They believe that sexual pleasure comes from outside stimulation and all the strategies and "have to's" that come with it.

The fact is, there is always sensation available in our bodies. When we become aware of those pleasurable sensations that are already present, we can close the gap quite easily. With a bit of practice, you are already "simmering," and when you want to engage sexually, the heat just needs to be turned up instead of trying to start from icy cold.

The following exercise can be done formally at first. Take ten to fifteen minutes a day to focus on specifically locating and widening pleasurable sensations. As you become familiar with the mechanics of this, you can engage in it anytime throughout your day, or in a more specific form when you get ready to engage sexually.

Background Pleasure Practice

Lie on your back on a comfortable, flat surface. Allow yourself to feel where your body connects with the ground. Then, as you begin to move your body subtly, bring your attention to any area in the body that already feels pleasurable and alive. If you like, you can stretch, or move your hands over your body, locating any area that feels good, and then focus on that area. Move in ways that keep that area alive, and take your time connecting with positive sensations in your body. If you can't feel any pleasure or aliveness, focus on an area where there is an absence of pain.

Let yourself enjoy the pleasurable areas and experiment with motions that support the well-being and aliveness you feel. See if you can spread the pleasant sensations through other parts of your body. If you lose the sensation, or it diminishes, find a different area that feels good and continue. Over time, you will learn to identify pleasurable sensations that are always there. You can sit on your desk and, for a moment, feel your shirt moving over your shoulders and enjoy the gentle sensation of a caress, or feel your hair moving over your neck and let that sensation spread down your arms.

Background pleasure is always available to keep you sensually awake and alive.

Over time, you will learn to identify pleasurable sensations that are always there. You can sit on your desk and, for a moment, feel your shirt moving over your shoulders and enjoy the gentle sensation of a caress, or feel your hair moving over your neck and let that sensation spread down your arms.

Sexual Pleasure Explorations

For women to be sexually alive and empowered, it is useful to spend some time with our own bodies, exploring sexual pleasure by ourselves. Learning and staying connected to the changing landscape of our arousal and knowing our bodies' pleasure maps are important aspects in staying connected to our feminine nature. Sexual pleasure generates energy and creates power. Aliveness and creativity result from engaging with the pleasure centers of our body.

Sexual pleasure generates energy and creates power. Aliveness and creativity result from engaging with the pleasure centers of our body.

Orgasms are not the goal here. Some women have them, some don't. Every woman and every situation is different. Scientists claim that some women can't have them, while most female sexual educators believe that every woman is capable of feeling many layers of pleasure, arousal, and climax when the circumstances are right, and when she is taught to feel her own body and learn her arousal patterns and circuits. I will discuss orgasms in more detail in the next chapter (chapter 10: "Orgasm," pp. 131–38). For the sake of our exploration, the following self-pleasure practice can, but does not have to, result in orgasm.

Self-Pleasure, Delocalized

Take some time and start touching your body. Focus first on your feet, massaging and pleasurably touching them, exploring sensations of pleasure as you work your way up around the ankles and calves, spending some time caressing the soft spots behind the knees, gradually making your way over the inner thighs toward your genitals. Take as much time as you can to feel how your body reacts to touch. Do you need to press into an area of tension to enjoy sensation? Or does a feather-light touch on the inside of the thighs heighten your sensations? Perhaps you feel quite numb—just stay with the exploration until you find an area that responds pleasurably. Note the different qualities of sensation, and over time, experiment with touch on all the different parts of the body so you have a complete map of sensations available to you. Focus on genital stimulation only when your whole body is awakened. If you start feeling that your attention and the sensation becomes too localized, go back to the whole body. Use this time to experiment and explore, instead of trying to achieve a goal.

Capacity

Once you have an established pleasure practice, you can play with your pleasure threshold by setting a timer and staying with the various stimulations for a bit longer than you usually would. It's interesting to notice when you have had enough, when you get bored, and when sensation diminishes. We tend to have an upper threshold for how much pleasure we can sustain, generally determined by factors such as previous positive and negative experiences, how much pleasure we generally feel, habits, and social/religious conditioning.

Capacity for pleasure can be increased through practice and inquiry, the same way a muscle can be trained or a skill can be learned. And that means practice, repetition, and finding out what blocks you from developing a greater capacity. As in a workout, it will become abundantly clear what the blocks are once you are doing the exercise—the key here being that the discovery as well as the increase in capacity will come from engaging with the pleasure practice. Easy, right? Everyone wants more pleasure, right? Well, you will find out by doing this exercise.

Capacity Exercise

Determine a length of time that is a bit beyond what you usually allot for self-pleasure. Set a timer and stay with giving yourself pleasure for as long as the time is set. Do not stop because you are tired, bored, or already had an orgasm. Boredom and sudden feelings of tiredness are often a sign of resistance, a way to get out of the actual exploration. Notice what happens when you stay with the sensations of pleasure as a discipline. There is no right or wrong way to experience self-pleasure, but there are conditionings and barriers that prevent us from feeling as much and as fully as we could. This exercise is a good way to explore and expand.

10

Orgasm

WOMEN'S ORGASMIC PLEASURE OCCUPIES PRIDE OF PLACE AMONG ALL the various controversial women's topics today.

There are still widespread differences and misunderstandings in its definition, as well as what types of orgasms truly exist. There are scientific studies that deny the existence of the G-spot, while in many sacred sexuality circles, the experience of the clitoral orgasm is maligned as unspiritual and inferior.

Wherever we turn, from the cover of *Cosmopolitan* to hands-on sex education courses, orgasm is still considered the Holy Grail of women's accomplishment.

Naturally, enjoying orgasms is not only extremely pleasurable, it also has incredible physical and mental health benefits. However, the commonly used phrase of "achieving orgasm" epitomizes the issue of characterizing the delicate unfolding of pleasure in a woman's body as a high-performance sport.

Adding to these pressures of orgasm are the exaggerated depictions of what women's pleasure looks like, both in mainstream movies and TV shows, as well as in actual porn. Add to this the current emphasis on so-called Tantric techniques that are supposed to help us to have multiple kinds of distinctly different orgasms, and we find ourselves in a veritable orgasmic arms race.

Many women I have encountered in my work believe they need to be extremely skilled, loud, and multiorgasmic to be considered a "sexually liberated" woman. Often, we are insecure about our own experience and depth of pleasure and what this means for our value as a sexual partner, and as a woman. Sadly, this often extends to our sexual intimacy with a partner, causing everything from unnecessary insecurity to faked orgasms to prove how highly responsive and orgasmic we are, to dissatisfaction with our partner's performance.

When it comes to orgasms, the less internal and external pressure there is to perform, the more likely it is that pleasure will result. When it comes to intimacy with a partner, trust and relaxation are much bigger contributing factors than actual technique. When we pleasure ourselves, doubt, performance anxiety, and excessive thought diminish our ability to feel pleasure. Understanding and being sensitive to the feelings of our bodies creates stronger pleasure than any fancy technical application.

My experience in working with women has shown that relaxation and sensitization are the most important aspects that lead to fulfilling orgasmic pleasure. How we perceive orgasms has much to do with how much we can feel in our bodies, as discussed in the previous chapter on pleasure (chapter 9: "Pleasure Is Our Birthright," pp. 113–129).

....

My experience in working with women has shown that
relaxation and sensitization are the most important
aspects that lead to fulfilling orgasmic pleasure.

....

Some women orgasm easily, with and without a partner; some only in one very specific way; others report they have never experienced orgasm, but that they experience intense full-body aliveness and pleasure. The orgasmic experience is as varied as women themselves.

There are a variety of educational books on the many kinds of orgasms, and the techniques and toys that can help us to experience them on our own or with a partner.

For the sake of this book, I am focusing on women's empowerment, which I believe comes from being able to explore and give ourselves the various kinds of pleasure available to us. I am a firm believer that knowing our bodies and being able to pleasure ourselves is an important aspect of being empowered women.

By exploring our bodies and the different ways to pleasure ourselves, we connect with yet another aspect of bodily wisdom and a treasure trove of sensations. We become sexually self-sufficient, which makes us less likely to engage in harmful relational and sexual behavior. And even if we are in a sexual relationship, we come from a place of "full" rather than a place of need and lack, which allows for a much richer and deeper intimacy.

....

By exploring our bodies and the different ways to pleasure
ourselves, we connect with yet another aspect of bodily
wisdom and a treasure trove of sensations. We become
sexually self-sufficient, which makes us less likely to
engage in harmful relational and sexual behavior.

....

With this in mind, I am describing a few different kinds of orgasm here. This is by no means a comprehensive list; rather, it is meant as an invitation to explore, should you feel interested in doing so. There are good anatomical charts, detailed instructions, and a myriad of anatomically appropriate wands available elsewhere should you wish to explore further on your own.

Clitoral Orgasm

The clitoris, being partly external, is easy to access and stimulate. Clitoral arousal is characterized as localized and external. Climax is usually accompanied with a tensing of the body, especially the pelvic area, thighs, and belly. The orgasm is short and intense and results in pelvic contractions. Often the climax also results in an emotional release. Most women report that after the orgasm, they need a break before they can become aroused again.

Explore

Most woman have a well-established way of creating clitoral arousal. Experiment with changing those touch and movement patterns. Try using the nondominant hand, a different speed, a lighter or heavier touch than usual, or a different position. Notice the change in quality of sensation and add these new approaches and sensations to your pleasure repertoire.

G-spot Orgasm

The G-spot is often described as a ribbed, coin-size area on the anterior wall of the vagina, two to three inches inside. While this is a helpful description in terms of locating a region to explore, many women have reported that they were not able to locate the G-spot until they were aroused.

Often the first few times of stimulating the G-spot result in a mildly unpleasant sensation of having to pee, which is actually a sign that you have located the right area. The G-spot is sometimes described as a "spongy" area that can fill with fluids, causing arousal, and in some women, the release of fluids during orgasm.

The orgasm resulting from G-spot stimulation has a very different feel than clitoral release, and often women who are used to the intensity of clitoral orgasms find the dispersed sensations of G-spot orgasms less exciting.

To begin with, it might take a much longer time to orgasm, and not every woman experiences orgasm or squirting. Once we become accustomed to the different quality of this kind of orgasm, the sensations unfold with a deep and undulating quality, and our bodies are easily able to orgasm several times in a row without losing interest or arousal.

G-spot orgasm can be reached with training. With a bit of time and practice it becomes much more available and lends a whole new dimension to pleasure.

Explore

If you are new to G-spot pleasure, find a designated G-spot wand, which allows for a more relaxed exploration than using your hand. Begin to stimulate the general area once you are already aroused. Make sure you are in a comfortable, relaxed position, perhaps leaning back on a few pillows, so your body does not have to tense and contort. If you locate an area of heightened sensation, play with staying relaxed while you explore, not rushing, pushing, or clenching. Instead of focusing on climax, allow this exploration to be about finding different sensations and areas of pleasure. If you are experienced with your G-spot, explore how relaxed you can get. While you are stimulating the G-spot, notice areas of clench, contraction, and push, and dissolve those as much as possible. You can also play with duration, keeping up the stimulation a bit longer than you usually would, exploring your pleasure threshold.

Cervical Orgasm

The cervix is the entrance of the womb, and is often very sensitive to touch or contact. It is said that emotional hurt gets stored on and around the cervix, and by touching and subsequently stimulating the cervix, we can release those old stored emotions. Many women find the area to be anywhere from lightly sensitive to extremely painful to the touch. With careful stimulation over time, the area can become very pleasurably enlivened, and eventually, cervical orgasms can occur.

Most women report that the prerequisite for cervical orgasms is a feeling of openness and relaxation, and that the orgasm itself feels like a wave of pleasure moving through the whole body, with the aftereffects sometimes lasting hours or even days. There is a strong emotional component to the cervical orgasm experience. For some women, the sensation has an expansive quality far beyond physical pleasure, and many report a feeling of emotional well-being and openness afterwards.

Explore

If you are new to cervical stimulation, use a wand and very gently explore the area around the cervix, making sure to take your time. If you encounter sensitive areas, back off enough to avoid clenching or flinching, but keep on exploring the sensations that arise. Take your time; it might take weeks or even months until the area becomes enlivened and pleasurable. Notice the emotional quality of the sensations arising and let yourself be curious about each sensation, regardless of whether or not you consider them to be conventionally arousing. Trace the ripples of sensation through your relaxed body, noticing any new sensations and reactions you can feel.

....

> Notice the emotional quality of the sensations arising and let yourself be curious about each sensation, regardless of whether or not you consider them to be conventionally arousing. Trace the ripples of sensation through your relaxed body, noticing any new sensations and reactions you can feel.

....

If you are already experienced with G-spot orgasms, you can play with locating your cervix and its sensations while simply sitting, or even moving, without any direct touch. At first, simply sit and locate your cervix by feeling inward and by visualizing. You can lightly move your pelvis, or simply energetically engage with the area. Once you can locate your cervix, you can play with keeping awareness on it throughout your day and increasing the sensation into ripples of pleasure.

Full-Body Orgasm

Some women experience nonlocalized, full-body pleasure, sometimes even unrelated to sexual stimulation. This might happen while dancing, soaking in a bathtub, or simply during relaxation. Several of my clients report waking up from deep, restful sleep in a state of heightened full-body pleasure, and one woman in my workshops reports that she experienced this state during childbirth.

While most women have experienced states of pleasure without direct stimulation, very few have consistent access to pleasurable body aliveness. Habitual tension and stress keep us from experiencing the fullness of sensation that is always available in our bodies. By engaging with relaxation and sensitization, we activate our awareness of background pleasure. You will find further related exercises in section IV: "Sacred Practices of the Wild Woman," pp. 197–236.

Explore

While you are experiencing pleasure, notice the areas of your body that are alive and filled with sensation. Enjoy those areas of heightened sensation and allow yourself to relax into, rather than clench on to, the pleasurable feelings. Over time, this will increase your body's capacity for pleasure.

By connecting with our bodies and the different kinds of sensations and orgasms we are capable of experiencing, we not only take control of our own pleasure, but also prepare ourselves for deeper sexual intimacy with our chosen partner. The key is to enjoy the exploration rather than feel compelled to achieve a prescribed outcome. Your body is capable of immense pleasure, and wondrous sensations are always there to be explored!

11

The Wise Woman

AT A RECENT WOMEN'S EVENT, MANDY, A NEW PARTICIPANT, ASKED ME, "What is the function of an older woman beyond her childbearing age?"

Mandy told us that she was in her eighties, had lived a full life, experienced a marriage, raised several children, and had a successful artistic career. She had practiced yoga for many years, and her body and mind were vibrant and agile.

She told us that she had recently retired, gone through some physical challenges, and had come to my workshop with this specific question in mind, wanting to explore what to do next with her life.

My first answer to her question was "Wisdom." We then spoke about passing on the knowledge that can only be gained from experiencing life, the challenges of aging as a woman, and the inevitable loss of people we love.

In a society where female youth and beauty are valued almost above all else, becoming an older woman is difficult, even for the most robust and fulfilled woman.

Even though many women I spoke with have expressed great relief and reported a sense of renewed energy and freedom after menopause, most report that the transition period proved challenging as they adjusted to a marked change in the way they were perceived and treated.

How much women are affected by this transition depends on how strongly they identified with their looks as a form of validation. Women who strongly identified with being sexually desirable and using their attractiveness to navigate life had a much harder time with the inevitable transition.

We are told that what men value in women is youth, fertility, and radiance. The beauty industry is geared toward supplying us with products that aid in radiant skin, glossy hair, and shiny white teeth. Bras and compression garments provide help with the perfect figure, plastic surgery offers a solution for any kind of sagging, and now almost everything can be resurfaced by lasers.

Regardless, at some point the looks will go and what is left depends on how much the women have engaged in their inner lives. The deeply attractive qualities of "a woman of a certain age" are confidence, substance, experience, and an inner radiance that comes from a life well lived and a heart well given.

....

> The deeply attractive qualities of "a woman of a certain age"
> are confidence, substance, experience, and an inner radiance
> that comes from a life well lived and a heart well given.

....

In indigenous cultures, elders are revered for their experience, their insight, and their ability to offer a bigger-picture view of life. Often, the matriarch of a family or tribe is consulted and makes decisions on all important matters.

Becoming the Wise Woman is a position that can't be bought, faked, or trained for. The only way to reach it is by staying alive long enough. There are lessons that can be learned only through the insight of hindsight, and a certain surrender and softness that comes from having loved, and lost, and loved again.

Becoming the Wise Woman is a position that can't be bought, faked, or trained for. The only way to reach it is by staying alive long enough. There are lessons that can be learned only through the insight of hindsight, and a certain surrender and softness that comes from having loved, and lost, and loved again.

After speaking with Mandy, I became acutely aware that I am about to enter the same territory. It's not as clear-cut for me, perhaps, since I have taught, consulted clients, and given counsel since my thirties, and so the role of adviser is well known to me. Aging and its resulting insights and losses, on the other hand, are a new exploration.

I can't say that I have made peace with this process, or that I have some handy tips or definitive answers I can share here with you. I do feel that this is a deeply personal and individual exploration that every woman has to face. I can, however, say that for myself and the women I have worked with, it is a worthwhile and, at times, vulnerable yet inevitable process that brings depth and growth, reshapes priorities, and lends itself to a softening and surrender.

While speaking with a friend about this chapter, we laughed about some of the statements we made in our thirties. It is easy to proclaim that one will age gracefully, not resort to youth-prolonging remedies—and secretly look down on women who have done so—when everything is still in its proper place and has its proper color, and aging is an interesting, almost exotic consideration.

Not so easy when the woman in the mirror looks nothing like what I remembered, or when recovery after demanding travel takes much longer than before, or when circles that appear under my eyes after a long night no longer go "back to normal," and gray appears around my temples.

It's not so easy when hormonal changes are not just a concept one teaches about in a women's group but something one begins to experience firsthand. And these are just the superficial outward tell-tale signs that announce to the world that I am now of a "certain age."

Some days I surrender to this process with good humor and a beautiful relaxation, and other days I vacillate between strong denial and abject panic. I have caught myself proclaiming to my mirror image: "Remember, this is the best you are ever going to look," and then laughed or cried hysterically—depending on the day.

I once mentioned something along these lines in a Facebook post and was blindsided by some reactions that felt like an odd sort of "love and light" reverse ageism. Some women even commented that they felt sorry for me that I felt this way and gave me admonishments on how I should embrace my beauty regardless of the demands of the patriarchy— that I was beautiful and vibrant regardless, and should stop shaving and painting my toenails.

I must say that looking down onto my bright pink toenails gives me great pleasure, and the condition of my armpits is my personal business altogether. I have never been that concerned with the patriarchy or the demands of men; however, for me, the state of my face, body, and health is a deeply personal exploration, one that requires speaking with actual honesty about what's happening in order not to bypass or obsess on these matters.

Much more interesting and complicated within this aging process is my inner life. During the writing of this book, just a short week ago, I turned fifty. My birthday made me feel both proud of having lived an incredibly rich life so far, and astounded that half a century has passed.

I have never actually felt more vital, creatively alive, and happy than I do now. In many ways, I feel much stronger, more confident, and mentally sharp than I ever have. I do feel more freedom than ever before. The author Isabel Allende expresses this beautifully in her TED Talk on aging: "I don't have to prove anything anymore. I'm not stuck in the idea of who I was, who I want to be, or what other people expect me to be."[7]

At the same time, there are recent realizations about things I definitely will never experience—or never experience again. For my whole adult life, I have lived in the possibility of vast potential. Everything was possible. I could choose between so many paths and motivated myself with the many opportunities I had not yet explored. Of course, I still have many of these opportunities, but the ones connected with time, sexual viability, fertility, and privilege based on my youth, looks, and vitality are gradually waning.

I am discussing these considerations not from a place of "woe is me" but as an attempt to be both frank and realistic. One could say that for every opportunity no longer available, another door opens. As much as this is true, there is also the fact that, as we grow older, some options do narrow.

Many years ago, I attended a presentation for hospice workers and volunteers. The speaker handed out index cards and asked us to write the ten activities and things we enjoyed most in our lives. Once we had our stack of cards ready, he narrated a story of the decline that happens when people get old and/or ill and eventually enter hospice. He asked us to imagine ourselves as the protagonist of that story. While he spoke he intermittently asked us to give up one card. We could choose which one was appropriate for the story, but as the illness progressed we had to let go of activities, hobbies, work, and friends we had listed. I never forget the moment when all I had left was one card that said "my dogs" as he narrated entering hospice and having to leave the last card behind.

The exercise impacted me deeply and made me cherish the abilities and opportunities I have presently. It also gave me a different perspective on the activities of my aging parents and a deeper compassion for the elderly in my community.

In the same TED Talk, Isabel Allende echoes this when she speaks about how it scares her that she is slowly losing her independence at age seventy-one, while inside she still feels like a sexy, seductive twenty-one-year-old.[8]

This exercise is at the extreme end of things to consider, but long before we reach assisted living or hospice care, there are subtle changes in how we are perceived and how we see ourselves. I am not even addressing the bodily shifts caused by changing hormone levels here, but they certainly add extra "flavor" to the considerations.

Even though I have consciously chosen not to have children, it is one thing to choose, quite another to no longer have a choice. Knowing how to make myself invisible when walking in an airport or through a crew of construction workers—a skill I was very proud of—is very different than just plain being invisible.

Within the last three years, I have been given the task of holding the lineage of my teacher. To begin with, this held little weight. But over the course of a few months, and combined with some other considerations, it became very clear to me that I did not have endless time. Through the lens of having to find at least one successor and train her sufficiently to carry the lineage forth, my activities—both personal and professional—have taken on an urgency, and my priorities have had to be restructured.

I realized that I had to start teaching in more depth, not only as a way to give people an experience, but in a way that gave them education, insight, and knowledge that they themselves could pass on. I felt a strong sense of responsibility to do so, knowing that I probably would want to keep up the enormously fast pace I am now enjoying only for a few more years. I became aware that holding on to my knowledge and doling it out in bits and pieces was no longer appropriate.

At the same time, my awareness of people and situations that sucked up my energy was suddenly heightened. My boundaries became increasingly clear, as I did not want to spend time on people or projects that kept me from giving what there still is to give. As a result, I have more energy and available creativity than ever before.

This brings me back to the wider considerations around aging. In the conversation with Mandy, we spoke at length about having to find things to source from other than beauty, sexual attractiveness, and youth.

When those things go, as they inevitably will for all of us who are privileged to live long enough, there have to be other skills and attributes on which to rely, such as humor, gained from the knowledge that some things, as hard as one may try to influence them, will never change; or relaxation, from knowing that not everything needs to be done perfectly and that one's worth is not connected to how much we get done; resourcefulness and flexibility; fortitude, from having our hearts broken and still deciding to love again and again; vibrancy and confidence; sexual maturity, from having relaxed enough to feel our own bodies deeply; generosity, not as a martyr but because, why not!; aliveness; and wisdom, gained from having survived as long as we have.

The Wise Woman is an interesting archetype to consider. When we look at representations of the archetype across different cultures, we see every role, from a leathery old granny to a wildly powerful shamanness.

To me, the Wild Woman naturally develops into the Wise Woman. With experience, all the open, connected, and intuitive parts of us come into full play within the context of passing on wisdom and well-earned knowledge.

The Wise Woman's greatest promise is that she is free: free from the considerations that come with having and rearing children, free from societal constructs, and free from self-imposed constraints. She can be a medicine woman, a sorceress, a healer, an artist, or pursue whatever form her freedom might take. She can enjoy spending time and energy on herself and her own pursuits and guide others through places they have not yet been.

> The Wise Woman's greatest promise is that she is free: free from the considerations that come with having and rearing children, free from societal constructs, and free from self-imposed constraints.

With age comes acceptance. With acceptance comes a certain relaxation. Anyone who has engaged in life long enough has encountered the inevitable moment when things, despite all our best efforts, fall apart. We experience breakups, death, illnesses, and failure. We are confronted with the inevitability of everything coming to an end. Regardless of how much we try, things don't always work out.

There are also sudden touches of grace, luck that comes out of nowhere, miracles and ecstatic moments that sear themselves into our hearts. There is no way of telling what is what, so eventually we realize that everything is the gift of being fully alive.

At the moment of surrender, a whole new landscape reveals itself, full of possibilities and connections that bring everything into a new, sharp focus, with a heart both tenderized and open, ready to engage with whatever may come.

Mandy has since decided to mentor young women in the arts and pass on some of the lessons she learned as an artist. She continues to practice yoga every day and jokes that she might try her hand at Tinder before her ninetieth birthday.

In a recent interview, I was asked what advice I would give my twenty-year-old self. After a moment of laughter, I told the interviewer that my twenty-year-old self would not have listened to me. Nonetheless, here are the somewhat random pieces of advice that I would offer her and have offered to some of my students and clients:

- Always wear sunscreen on your chest.
- Revel in your body!
- Dress for your own enjoyment.
- Don't waste time on a man who won't commit.
- Always floss your teeth.
- Have some good fun and travel before you enter the competitive world of career and the pursuit of accomplishments.
- Remember that everything you do accumulates into habit patterns over time.
- Smile.

- Be generous.
- Spend time with your parents. If your relationship is not good—fix it or move on.
- Find someone you trust to give you reflection and support.
- Invest in a high-quality pair of sunglasses and wear them.
- Move your body as much as possible.
- Love deeply, regardless of the consequences.

III

The Untamed Heart

12

Dating

REBECCA JUST COULD NOT UNDERSTAND WHY SHE WAS SINGLE AGAIN!
At thirty-five, she thought she had found her man and had put all her effort into creating the perfect relationship. Alternately sobbing and ranting, she told our women's group how much Robert had changed for the better over the last year. She recounted how she had helped him renovate his place, picked out trendier clothes for him, and even encouraged him to try for a different position at his company. He really was becoming the man she knew he could be.

She was sure he was going to propose for her birthday. And then he broke up with her! "How could he not want to be with me?" she sobbed. Smart, beautiful, and accomplished, she ran her own business and made good money. She knew how to treat a man right and gave him a lot of freedom and even encouraged him to go out and have drinks with his friends. She considered herself the perfect catch.

Other women in the circle nodded compassionately, adding similar stories of dating and breakups. Why, Rebecca asked, was it so hard to find a man who wanted to commit to her?

After asking a few specific questions, my answer to Rebecca's conundrum was an inconvenient one. Rebecca had the habit of dating men with "potential."

Here is the dictionary definition of "potential": having or showing the capacity to become or develop into something in the future. She was dating a man who one day could be what she knew he was capable of. Not yet, but soon—and with a little help from her, of course!

She saw Robert's potential and did whatever she could to help him become the man she wanted him to be. There is a problem with this, though. The Robert she met and the man he was throughout the relationship was never good enough for her. He was not tidy enough, his apartment was not modern enough, his clothes were not trendy enough, his job was not up to her standards.

Robert was simply a commodity for Rebecca. She tried to mold him to her needs, attempting to make Robert fulfill her fantasies of what her husband would be like. She did not see the man Robert truly was. As Robert pointed out when he broke up with her, he felt as if he were a Ken doll she dressed up—made to move the way she wanted him to.

To make matters worse, her support of him, in her words, "growing and becoming the man she knew he could be," had the flavor of an indulgent mother, not that of a girlfriend cheering on a man she was proud of to begin with.

Her "allowing" him to go for drinks with his friends, the way she picked out his clothes and inquired about his career plans, had a quality of subtle superiority. She knew what was best for him and her support came with a healthy dose of disapproval when he did not comply with her suggestions.

For a while, Robert did his best to please her, but he eventually decided to move on because, as he told her, he felt like he could not do anything right and she was impossible to please.

Rebecca's story is a common one. Many women have the innate ability to look at people and see their potential. We love to help, heal, and support. It feels natural to use our talents and gifts to make life better for those we love. Some women extend that talent even to fixer-upper houses, failing businesses, or in my case, homeless dogs.

The problem with dating men with potential is that they are not who we want them to be . . . yet. And, as with Robert, this means that we disapprove of who they actually are now. The male-to-female equivalent of a woman saying about a man, "He is great, broke at the moment and just needs to dress a bit better, and with my help he'll have an amazing job soon" is: "She is cool; if she loses twenty pounds, changes her hair color, and gets a boob job, she will be perfect."

It's painful for both men and women to be with someone who fundamentally does not agree with who we are right now. If you are actively dating, it is important that you are clear on your present-day requirements in a man, as well as honest in your assessment of your own talents and attributes.

Dating in this day and age is a difficult process as it is. Navigating Tinder, Bumble, and the more conventional dating sites and creating online profiles seems like a full-time job. For many women, meeting men who are looking for more than just casual dating and convenient sex requires good instincts and, more importantly, a solid idea of what they actually want out of a relationship.

There are many good coaches who can guide you through the dating process, but before you start dating, there are a few bigger-picture aspects of dating to consider:

Clarify what kind of relationship you want.

Every intimate relationship has a purpose. Depending on where you are in your life, that could be anything from occasional casual fun to marriage and children. Sure, you don't know how it will turn out when you start dating, but ideally you do know where you want to go if all goes well.

In my work, I often see couples who have never discussed the purpose of their relationship, and frequently, their conflicts stem from assumed common goals and misaligned relational intentions.

....

> In my work, I often see couples who have never discussed the
> purpose of their relationship, and frequently, their conflicts stem
> from assumed common goals and misaligned relational intentions.

....

For instance, when the purpose of a relationship is having and raising children, this takes priority over an active travel or social life for a while. If a couple prioritizes fun, sex, and travel and suddenly one of the two wants to settle down and have children, it will require a change in purpose for both partners.

The purpose of a relationship can change, for instance when the children leave the house, but the change needs to be discussed and adjusted to.

The landscape of relationship has changed dramatically over the past ten years. There are many more options available to us in terms of the type of relationship we can have. Some people want long-term commitment but not marriage; some want children, some don't; some already have children; some want a primary partner and other less-committed relationships available to them. There is the option of long distance, separate bedrooms, separate houses, communal living, alternative lifestyles of all kinds, and every kind of sexual and relational consideration imaginable. You can no longer assume that someone out there dating wants what you have in mind.

Before you engage with anyone, you might want to feel and think through what you truly require from a relationship. Many woman subconsciously cling to the fairy-tale ideal, but when they really examine their lives and what they are reasonably able to commit to, this ideal is a far cry from what they can really show up for. Others believe that they are perfectly open to the casual connection they agreed to, while their heart yearns for deep, lasting commitment.

For this, take an honest look at where you are and the trajectory of your life. Imagine where you'd like to be in two, five, and ten years. What are the aspects of life that you absolutely want to experience, taking into account your personal life goals, your career plans, and whether or not you want children? If you are considering dating at the point in your life where biological children are no longer an option, consider whether or not you want a relationship that includes children and family from a partner's previous marriage or relationship.

....

Imagine where you'd like to be in two, five, and ten years. What are the aspects of life that you absolutely want to experience, taking into account your personal life goals, your career plans, and whether or not you want children?

....

Be clear how much time you want to—and realistically can—spend with a future partner. Assess your lifestyle requirements and have your "no-go's" honestly defined. The more clarity you have, the better you can define what you are looking for in a partner.

Define the qualities of the partner who fits this kind of relationship.

Once you are clear on the relationship you want and, most importantly, the kind that you can honestly enter and sustain, define the kind of partner who would be willing and capable of joining you. This is where the commitment not to date "potential" comes in.

If you know you want children, don't consider a man who is unsure and think, "Oh, he will want to have children when we know each other better." Don't anticipate that you will "turn him around" on any issue, for that matter. If he says he does not want to do something—regardless of what that is—assume that this is 100 percent true. The same applies if he himself has aspirations. Don't assume that because he has a goal, he will reach it. In your mind, imagine whether you would still want to be with him if he never reached his stated goal.

If you have any expectations that he will grow into his potential, back off! He might, but he might not, and in the meantime, while you are waiting, you are depriving him of having a partner who truly likes and accepts him for who he is, and depriving yourself of the partner you desire.

Clarify who you are and what you have to offer this kind of partner.

Take a good, honest look at who you are. Be realistic with what you have achieved so far and what you are hoping for. Here is a list of questions you can consider. If you have a trusted friend who can give you a frank outside view, these are questions you can ask him or her.

- Do you know what you want from a partner and from a relationship?
- Are you equipped to sustain what you desire?
- Are your life, habits, and surroundings conducive to the kind of intimacy you want?
- What do you have to offer a partner?
- Is your life a mess, and do you want a partner to rescue you?

- Do you believe that once you are in a relationship, your life will be magically transformed?
- Are you ready to receive what you desire right now?

Consider these questions and examine any myths of Prince Charming still lurking in your mind. Chances are that if you need a man to fix you and support your life, one of several things will happen:

1. **The kind of partner who truly could support you will not be attracted to you.** Quality men do not want to date needy women. Constant drama and breakdowns are not interesting to a loving and stable man who wants to create a full and successful life.

2. **You'll find a "savior" and enter into a codependent relationship.** Men who fancy themselves as "white knights" tend to create unhealthy entanglements, as they derive their worth from rescuing you, not from relating to you as an equal partner.

3. **You'll fall for a promise that is never fulfilled, and you will chase that potential endlessly.** You saw a glimpse of his best, but he never quite connected as deeply again. You spend the rest of the relationship chasing the ghost of that intimacy.

This is not to say that, in a good relationship, both partners don't contribute and support each other; but they do so ideally from a place of mutual ability and generosity, and not because one partner's life, mood, or career is constantly falling apart.

This might sound harsh, but consider that as women we have certain time limitations on our fertility that we must take into consideration in our choices around career and life timing. You do not want to waste your time and energy and spend years of your life with partners who are not a good fit. It's not fair to you or to them.

As you consider dating and entering a relationship, focus first on who you are, what you have to offer, and what you honestly desire from a partner. If you find that you are unclear about what you want or what you can offer, or that you have areas in your life that need work, spend some time and energy exploring first. Coming from a place of clarity, honesty, and self-worth will give you a good chance of finding someone with whom you are compatible and can enjoy the fullness of intimacy.

13

Relationships

PAUL AND LISA SAT ON MY OFFICE COUCH CLOSE TOGETHER, LISA tenderly patting Paul's arm as they tried to decide who would speak first. At first glance, they appeared connected and considerate of each other. However, as they told their story, a slightly different picture began to emerge.

The couple had met four years before in a yoga class and took their relationship from dating to living together within six months. Lisa, in her mid-thirties, had felt that she had no time to lose on long "trial relationships" and that her connection to Paul was so immediate and intimate that she had no doubts about committing to him and the relationship.

Paul described how their sexual connection had been so electric that for the first few months they barely went out. Then, gradually, as they went on to move in together, they developed a thriving social life, spending their free time inviting friends for dinners and attending events and yoga weekends together.

After two years, they decided to turn their mutual love for yoga and exercise into a business and started an online company together. They were currently working together from their home and spent all day on the business together.

They both emphasized how wonderful their relationship was, except for one problem. They did not feel like being intimate anymore. It had been six months since they had last had sex, and every time they attempted to make time for intimacy, neither of them felt like engaging, and they would just watch TV or fall asleep instead.

Neither of them could understand why this was happening. After all, they loved each other, had a great time together, and were very physically affectionate. As a matter of fact, the whole time they were talking to me, they were touching each other in some way.

As we started exploring the issue, Lisa's mood became resentful. She felt rejected by Paul and expressed that she was overworked and in her head, and if he would make the first move, she would probably be able to respond sexually. Paul replied by detailing the irritation Lisa expressed when he so much as hinted at any sexual engagement. He felt burdened by the responsibility of always having to make the first move, and then being rejected and made to feel he was lacking in manliness.

They had gone to relationship counseling before and had been advised by their therapist to spend time talking with each other and to make time for nonsexual touch, both of which led to even more expectation and frustration. The more time they spent together and the more they touched, the more they fell into what Lisa called a "buddy relationship." Neither of them felt erotic tension or the desire to take their interaction from the friendly touching to something sexier.

Paul and Lisa's story is one I have encountered many times, both in my private practice and in workshops. There are variations on the theme, but the underlying issue is the assumption that a good relationship makes for exciting sexual attraction.

The very aspects that make a relationship successful can harm your sex life if you are not aware that sexual attraction and a good loving relationship require diametrically opposite skills and behaviors. Relationship is built on sameness. Sexual excitement is created by difference. The more difference, the hotter the sex (as any woman who has ever dated "the wrong guy" knows).

What Makes a Good Relationship?

For a relationship to work, the more two people have in common, the better. Common goals, friends, interests, religious and political views, and day-to-day preferences make for a harmonious partnership.

When we first meet someone romantically, everything is fresh. Most of us remember the delicious first weeks of talking into the night, sharing history, opinions, and plans. We discover what we have in common, and it feels thrilling to discover a shared love of Italian food or an obscure favorite band.

During this phase of getting to know each other, there is so much to discover; sex feels exciting, the promise of deepening intimacy is thrilling, and the dynamics of the relationship are still being defined.

In this phase, the possibilities seem limitless. Long walks, weekends in bed, frequent texts and phone calls, and dates all feel like an adventure.

Then, over time, a couple does get to know each other. They develop routines, common friends and activities, and have heard all of each other's best and worst stories. Perhaps they move in together and spend more time together. The newness has worn off and, if all goes well, a harmonious relationship built on commonality sets in.

Often the relationship now involves the stress of day-to-day upkeep, a business, or children. At some point, the couples find themselves at home on a Saturday night, in sweatpants on the couch, watching their favorite show, lovingly touching, but with no sexual impetus or attraction whatsoever. The "spark" has gone.

The important thing to know here is the attraction having diminished is not the sign of the relationship failing. The lost spark is caused by commonality, familiarity, and too much time spent together without conscious purpose.

Most people, including some couples counselors, try to fix attraction issues with relationship solutions. This can be very counterproductive, causing frustration and discouragement.

....

> Most people, including some couples counselors, try to fix
> attraction issues with relationship solutions. This can be very
> counterproductive, causing frustration and discouragement.

....

Relationship issues are issues of not having enough in common. It could be that values and beliefs are not or are no longer aligning, or the partners have different lifestyles, different preferences around touch, sex, religion, money, and, most commonly, issues with communication—basically, all the things that in a divorce court fall under "irreconcilable differences."

Relationship issues can and should be addressed by a qualified therapist, who can mediate differences in values and contribution and teach communication skills. If common goals and values are no longer possible, a therapist can at least bring both parties into enough agreement to separate with a degree of civility.

Often people worry that when the sexual spark starts to wane in an otherwise healthy partnership, it's a sign of relationship trouble. Diminishing attraction left unattended too long, or not properly understood, can lead to relationship problems, but again, it's important to know that relating well and keeping the sexual spark alive are actually different issues with different solutions. This distinction alone has helped many of my clients immensely.

The Mechanics of Sexual Attraction

Sexual attraction follows very different principles from relationship. As noted earlier, while relationship is built on sameness, sexual attraction is based on difference. The stronger the difference and the further apart the two poles, the greater the sexual tension. This principle is sometimes called "sexual polarity," and in my lineage, it is called "erotic friction."

Erotic friction is a great term, as it indicates that the erotic hotness comes from friction, which can be seen as two different people coming together and polarizing instead of resonating for the sake of the erotic. Often, we see couples who have a contentious, explosive relationship but a great, active sex life.

So, does this mean that if you have a wonderful relationship you are doomed to eventually have boring sex and diminished attraction? The answer is yes and no.

It is not so easy to find someone with whom we can be compatible and have a harmonious, loving relationship, so the relationship aspect should always take precedence over all else. Reclaiming the spark, or even better, being preventative and keeping the spark alive, is much easier, as it is a set of mechanics and skills that can be learned. With some information and a bit of discipline, a couple can keep the attraction strong and alive throughout the relationship.

....

It is not so easy to find someone with whom we can be
compatible and have a harmonious, loving relationship,
so the relationship aspect should always take precedence
over all else. Reclaiming the spark, or even better, being
preventative and keeping the spark alive, is much easier, as
it is a set of mechanics and skills that can be learned.

....

In the Tantric lineage in which I was trained, the two poles are sometimes called "Shiva" and "Shakti," which in Western use is often translated into "masculine" and "feminine." These terms are a bit outdated to describe the principles of sexual attraction. People tend to conflate "masculine" with men and "feminine" with women, which is not an appropriate use and creates confusion, and at its worst, gender wars.

Each human being has an equal amount of masculine and feminine energy within them. We could simply call it "go" and "flow."

For any human being to function, both "go" and "flow" have to be available and engaged. "Go" is the ability to get things done, create structure, create and execute plans, and give direction to the flow of life. Equally, each human being needs to have "flow," which is the ability to be open, flexible, feeling and flowing with life itself in all its forms.

For the sake of sexual polarity, each partner takes on one pole. One partner offers "flow," the other one "go." In other words, one partner sexually invites and softens, while the other one energetically leads and creates structure. With each partner representing predominantly one aspect, difference is created. This difference makes for the spark, the erotic friction that creates sexual hotness.

We tend to have a preference; most people either prefer to be the one predominantly taking and penetrating, which is attributed to "go," or surrendering and being taken sexually, which is associated with "flow." Ideally, both partners can embody both aspects, but get to play mostly within their preference.

When partners spend too much time together and pursue the same goals, either in business, with children, or socially, they inevitably begin to resonate with each other. There is less and less difference, which, sexually speaking, causes a lack of erotic friction, and with that, a lack of spark.

....

When partners spend too much time together and pursue
the same goals, either in business, with children, or socially,

they inevitably begin to resonate with each other. There is
less and less difference, which, sexually speaking, causes
a lack of erotic friction, and with that, a lack of spark.

In addition, there is no more strong delineation of activities. If business dealings, catching up, discussions about errands, and relational conversation all flow together, there is no chance to develop erotic friction. Having a conversation about money is not meant to be sexy; neither is discussing who picks up more toilet paper. When these discussions are mixed in on a date night, it extinguishes the spark quickly.

For the sake of illustrating this, let's go back to Lisa and Paul. Lisa enjoys being the partner who is receptive and relaxed, and is hoping that Paul will initiate and get her out of her head. Paul enjoys being the one who initiates and gives direction to the sexual occasion.

However, in daily life, they cooperate on a business, the household, and various activities. They touch often and cuddle, even during meetings, as they did in my office. Their "date nights" often turn into business brainstorming sessions, and Lisa admits that, on occasion, she has interrupted Paul when he was kissing her to remind him of an e-mail that still needed to be sent.

Their bodies are no longer used to one of them leading and one of them following. Their minds have no discipline in separating business from leisure. Emotionally, they have become habituated to drawing comfort and reassurance from casual, unconscious touch.

In our session, I asked them at what point in their relationship they had felt the strongest attraction, and they both agreed that the first six months, before they moved in together, were incredibly erotically charged.

I guided them back to their behaviors during that time. They could clearly see that they separated activities distinctly during that time. Both would work separately, then go to their homes and prepare for their date. Paul would come up with fun places to go and arrange everything for the evening. Lisa took some time to disconnect from work, often dancing around her house in excitement while getting ready for their date.

Both would shower, primp, dress with care, and clean up their apartments in anticipation of coming back together. When they were together on their date, neither of them answered their phones or e-mails, and they spent focused time with each other, deeply engaged in intimacy. Each time they met, they had not seen each other for a few days, and they had plenty of interesting stories of their separate activities to share with each other.

As we uncovered those behaviors, it became clear to both Lisa and Paul how they had lost their spark.

By adapting the principles that created strong erotic friction during the "honeymoon" of dating to the reality of an existing partnership, Lisa and Paul learned that it is possible to deliberately renew attraction and erotic engagement by tapping into those principles that had worked in the beginning, yet had faded away with time.

Once they became aware of how much time they spent together, they changed their work routines. They scheduled meetings at the beginning and end of their workdays, and Lisa moved her desk out of the office into the den. Both felt a rise in productivity, but more importantly, they were excited to meet up for lunch after having spent time apart.

It took some discipline not to visit each other's room anytime either of them felt like connecting. They'd meet for tea in the kitchen, which felt like a fun rendezvous. After a while, they also spent some evenings by themselves or with a friend, coming back home with stories and updates to share. They started date nights again, but this time they prepared separately and met up only when they both were ready to leave.

Over the course of a few months, and with a few adjustments to fit their individual needs, the spark returned, and both Paul and Lisa reported that now their sexual intimacy had deepened even beyond their first "honeymoon" dating period. While the initial spark had been based on unfamiliarity, the intimacy they now shared included the fullness of their lives together, the strong bond they had created, and the excitement of a renewed sexual engagement.

Lisa and Paul reconnected and revived their sexual relationship, as have many other couples I've worked with, and so can you. With the help of a few simple changes to your activities, you will be able to shift how you relate to each other for the sake of bringing back the spark—or not losing it in the first place. Here's how:

Delineate Your Activities

Separate your activities and the different topics of your life, and create discipline around keeping them apart. Designate times to discuss money and logistics. Plan dates, travel, and excursions that are for romantic engagement only. Create outings with family and friends that are free of business or networking. Decide what activity has what purpose, and stick with it.

One practice I recommend to all couples is to have weekly agenda meetings, during which household issues, bills, travel, logistics, and such are discussed. Having the discipline to gather the many administrative issues into a dedicated discussion time, instead of bringing them up whenever they pop into your mind, makes a huge difference. You can compile a list, or send yourself or your partner an e-mail, but don't bring it up when it comes into your mind! Not only does this make a huge difference in the erotic realm, it is also an excellent tool for heightened productivity. Nothing is less sexy than a discussion about the gas bill during a romantic evening!

Spend Time Apart

Even if you are living together, take some time for yourself. Depending on the demands of your life, this might be anywhere from just a few minutes to several hours. The important thing is to create an opportunity to come back to yourself and feel who you are. If you have time, pursue your own interests, and leave the house by yourself.

Many couples I work with have separate rooms, if space allows, so they can have the things they love in their own space and take some time alone. Regardless of whether you go on a trip alone, spend an evening out with friends, or take ten minutes alone in the bath, you will come back to the relationship with renewed energy. Pursuing your own interests equips you with brand new information and new stories to tell.

Recharge with Activities that Bring You Back into Your Body

Take responsibility for your energy levels and your own pleasure. Don't expect your partner to get you out of your head or romance you to open your heart. Your partner is also busy and tired.

Before you come together for a romantic occasion, feel your own body and tend to yourself the way you would want your partner to tend to you. Have a bath, a nap, some exercise, massage your feet, sit and rest, or whatever you would do to prepare for an exciting date. Move your body in ways that bring you back to feeling and sensual awareness. Remember all the things you did for yourself when you were first sexual with your partner? Do those again and feel how that influences your outlook on your time together.

....

Before you come together for a romantic occasion, feel your own body and tend to yourself the way you would want your partner to tend to you. Have a bath, a nap, some exercise, massage your feet, sit and rest, or whatever you would do to prepare for an exciting date.

....

Be Considerate and Generous

Treat your romantic time together as you imagine your ideal fantasy scenario to be. Show up with energy to give instead of wanting to take. Come prepared to meet with your partner as your lover, not as a known commodity. Be curious about who they are; ask new questions instead of assuming you already know everything about them. See them with fresh eyes. Be ready to be surprised by who they are and to give of yourself, your time, energy, and attention, generously.

Play with Leading and Following

Here is a fun game to try for a date. One of you leads the whole date; the other follows. Whoever leads is in complete charge of absolutely everything. This includes activity, location, food, drink, timing and directions. Whoever leads is attempting to create the most exciting, delightful and fun-filled date possible. Whoever follows, goes along without giving negative feedback (of course, if you must set a boundary, do, but ideally let yourself be guided and enjoy not being in charge).

After the date, perhaps even the next day, you can exchange feedback and share experiences with each other. A good format is for each of you to answer the following questions for yourselves out loud, without responding to what your partner said:

1. What was your favorite part of the date?

2. What was your least favorite part of the date?

3. What else could your partner have done to make the date even better?

Then, on the next date, the other partner is in charge and offers the lead.

Stop Touching!

Now, I don't mean you should stop touching altogether, but there is an important distinction between conscious and unconscious touch that many couples overlook.

Pay attention to how often you touch your partner in a casual or unconscious way. I often see women pet their partners as if they were children or dogs. Sweet maybe, but definitely not sexy.

Conscious Touch Exercise

As an experiment, don't touch for a few hours before you get together romantically. Then touch with purpose, as lovers, not as casual buddies or parents. You can also set some time aside and experiment with various kinds of touch, and find out how each affects your partner erotically. An easy way to play with this is by using your nondominant hand to touch your partner on the arm. Touch their arm with one finger, very lightly. With each subsequent stroke, experiment with different motions, with speed, and with more and less pressure. See how light and subtle you can make the touch and still make it pleasurable. You can give feedback in the form of "yes" and "no" sounds and then switch, with the other partner trying out touch on you.

Give Each Other Space

When both partners have had busy days, and are coming together in the evening, give yourselves some space before you engage. Spend some time apart after work and don't go into exchanging information, complaining about your day, or discussing logistics immediately. If you are parents, take some time apart after the kids are in bed before you enter connection again. Again, separating activities and having breaks to connect with your body between activities is key here.

Date-Night Discipline

Most couples' lives are busy enough that they have to actually schedule time for sex and romance. Most people ideally want spontaneity and an element of surprise, but mostly, the demands of modern life are such that if you wait for the magic moment when all the stars align, sex could be a once in a millennium event.

Be realistic with your scheduling, and don't place unfair demands on yourself or your partner. It's highly unlikely you are going to feel like crazy hot sex a few hours after a demanding meeting or ferrying a small army of children to soccer practice.

Whatever you plan to do, the most important part is to be disciplined in your attention. Focus on each other, and try not to talk about business, kids, friends, bills, or other topics that have nothing to do with the erotic. Instead, connect with each other, praise each other, tell new stories, or reminisce about a great memory you share. Ask each other questions, and speak about things you consider sexy. And, for heaven's sake, stay off your phone!

By following these steps, your relationship will re-wild itself, meaning it will come into its natural balance. As you enliven the body, return to feeling, and use these skills, you'll be able to connect with your partner instinctively and use your bodies, hearts, and mind as you connect.

14

Tribe

ALL OF MY WOMEN'S EVENTS START WITH AN OPPORTUNITY FOR EACH
participant to introduce herself. Depending on the venue, we might sit
in chairs, or cushions on the floor, but always in a circle, so each woman
can see the others while she speaks about herself and her reasons for
attending.

It is always thrilling to enter the room and see everyone for the
first time. I am fortunate enough to have women of all ages, nationalities, and orientations attending my events, and it is not uncommon for
women to bring their daughters, their friends, and even their mothers.
Participants range in age from twenty all the way into their eighties.

I have taught all over Europe, the US, Canada, and Australia.
Though every country has a unique flavor of women, the introductions
always have the same elements and often the same stories.

Some women are thrilled to be there, some look apprehensive, some defensive, and there are always one or two who look aloof, holding themselves a bit distant from the others, as if they had ended up in the circle by accident.

One by one, the women introduce themselves, sharing their names, where they are from, what brought them to this event, and what they wish to experience. The first few women are usually matter-of-fact, saying only a few sentences about themselves. Then, as more women take their turns to speak, the initial shyness begins to melt, and the stories start to emerge: stories of love and loss, of triumph over illness and abuse. Deaths are mourned. Pregnancies are revealed. Affairs, new romances, and fantasies of divorce are confessed. Tissues are passed to someone who is crying, and riotous laughter is shared. Someone will talk about her mistrust of women, someone will exclaim her joy in being among women only. At some point, a woman will usually say something like "I feel like I have lived and felt everything that has been said so far, these are all my experiences and emotions, too," and everyone agrees.

A circle of women holds ancient magic. I don't mean that in the "New Age goddess sisterhood" understanding of such words, but in the sense that such circles are the oldest form of communion among women.

....

A circle of women holds ancient magic. I don't mean that
in the "New Age goddess sisterhood" understanding
of such words, but in the sense that such circles are
the oldest form of communion among women.

....

When I look around these circles, I can envision the same configuration in a cave, a clearing in the woods, a tent, or a longhouse, a circle of women talking while preparing food or medicine, working on baskets, hides, and looms, a circle where laughter, ritual, discussion, conflict, and song are all shared in community.

From the beginning of humanity, women collaborated, sharing food, ritual, and childcare as a way of culture. Men, for most of human history, have been outside of this circle, risking their lives by hunting, sacrificing themselves in defense of their dwellings, as well as exploring and discovering new resources for the benefit of the tribe.

As a woman, being part of the tribal construct was essential for survival. Younger women were taught life skills, from food preparation, healing and medicines, and initiations into womanhood to child-rearing and rituals. Childbirth was assisted by more experienced women. Children were watched and tended to not only by their mothers, but also by aunts, grandmothers, elder siblings, and cousins; all the women of the tribe contributed. The stories, history, and myths of the tribe were transmitted in these circles.

To this day, when women come together, the magic of this long-standing, shared cultural experience is effortlessly remembered when we sit together. Our bodies remember. We still resonate with one another. We learn about being a woman from other women. We find solace in shared stories and benefit from each other's experience.

Finding your "tribe" and enjoying the support that comes from being in the company of other women is more important than ever. We are no longer living in communities, and most of us are without the support of the women in our family. With our busy lives, many women are deprived of the regular in-person meetings with girlfriends and the seemingly mundane but deeply connective activities of past times. Facebook, Instagram, Snapchat, and e-mail have replaced actual exchange, and instead of talking on the phone, texting is the way we often communicate.

Only a generation or two ago, women would still cook together or sit on their porch shelling peas on a hot summer afternoon. Making jam, quilting circles, and Tupperware parties were the women's groups of our mothers. This is by no means to say that we should go back to the suppressed housewife days of the fifties, but there is a wisdom to engaging in simple, communal activities that allow bandwidth for connecting, sharing, and listening, and that are free from goal-oriented pushing.

These seemingly antiquated activities are just a portal into the magic that unfolds when women gather. The regular contact and immersion into community straightens us out. It allows us to work out how to behave with other women. There will be conflict and drama, as there is any time humans gather, but within the community, mutual care, basic decency, and trust can develop when there is a sense that the goals are shared—when we shuck the peas together, we are feeding the tribe. When we gather to give gifts to a mother who is expecting a child, we are supporting the well-being of the next generation. When we plant the garden together, we are ensuring our collective survival—as we are doing when we get together to share our stories, challenges, and joys.

My little town has a new craft store, the hipster kind, with artistic macramé wall hangings made from unbleached merino and hand-dyed skeins of wool that cost more than a small sheep. The store is lavishly decorated, with yarns, books, pottery, fabrics, and beautiful objects arranged on exquisite wooden tables. The whole store is a thing of beauty.

The store hosts knitting and craft workshops on weekends. When I stopped by, I was met by a group of women, huddled together on oversize sofas. There was instruction given, but mostly these women sat together, chatting and knitting in the most companionable and touching way.

There was, as in my groups, a mix of ages: several young, hip-looking girls; a dreadlocked hippie mom with a baby in a sling; one of our local farmers; several well-to-do local women in various stages of middle age; and the instructor, a regal woman in her seventies wearing a homemade outfit.

What struck me when I entered were the sounds and the feeling of the store. Like a beehive, there was a happy hum and a feeling of community. I could overhear the women sharing stories and making jokes, everyone content and enjoying themselves. The instructor told me that every weekend more women join, and some of them are now meeting regularly in their homes.

Coming together with women can take many forms: a casual cup of tea, sitting together and talking, preparing a meal, attending a book club, going to the baths, dancing, or gardening are all ways to connect. I held regular "women's group" meetings at my house for many years as a way to combat the isolation of living far from home in the crowded chaos of Hollywood. In the early days of the group, we would take turns, and each meeting a different woman would suggest an activity and topic. We learned how to make candles, crocheted tiny hats for a local children's hospital, made jam, belly danced, and wrote poetry under the guidance of whoever led the evening.

Over time, the meetings became more structured in order to accommodate specific needs around emotional release and embodiment, and to allow for sharing as the numbers of attendees increased. But really, all it takes to begin is for women to gather and take some time to let go of the habitual hustle. All else will unfold naturally.

The principle behind creating a "tribe" is gathering a group of women and joining together in a simple activity that allows the body and mind enough space to feel, relax, and connect. Most important is that there is no pressure, no goal, and enough time for everyone to connect. The power of simple exchange and collaboration is extraordinary and brings us the magic of our tribe.

. . . .

The principle behind creating a "tribe" is gathering a group of women and joining together in a simple activity that allows the body and mind enough space to feel, relax, and connect. Most important is that there is no pressure, no goal, and enough time for everyone to connect.

. . . .

And yet, for all this ancient collaboration, why are women so competitive with one another? Why is there the potential for gossip, backstabbing, and side-taking anytime women come together? Some claim it is a recent phenomenon, brought on by competing in the workplace and for the seemingly dwindling supply of "good men."

Some say we always had to compete for the best resources, which I believe to be true. My thought is that we always needed to compete for the most powerful mate and the best food supply, but once we had achieved our place in the tribe, the hierarchy and the strong need for collaboration in order to thrive kept competition in check. In a tribal situation you can't survive alone, which is a major motivation for agreeable behavior. The women in a tribal construct would become a self-regulating force, curbing the extremes of competitive or detrimental behavior. Through the mutual need for survival, conflicts needed to be worked out instead of being swept under the proverbial rug.

Now we think that we no longer need the support of a tribe and so all bets are off. We can walk away anytime. Individuality is not only cherished, but revered. The ability to take care of oneself and succeed has become a valued trait. Working things out takes time, energy, and the wisdom of someone—an elder or a shaman in the tribe—to keep conflict constructive. Those mechanisms are no longer readily available or cultivated.

In recent years, pop culture has glorified this female competition as entertainment. For "enjoyment" we are shown a group of women pitted against one another in fierce battle over an eligible bachelor, and shows like *The Real Housewives of [fill in the city of your choice]* have glorified and monetized cattiness.

Social media rewards the prettiest, hippest, curviest, bendy-est of them all with "likes," followers, and fame. In the workplace, competitiveness among women has become a much-discussed topic that has necessitated advice books with titles such as *Mean Girls at Work*,[9] *Working with Bitches*,[10] and *Tripping the Prom Queen*.[11]

Even though studies claim that men are more competitive than women, the same studies report that men are more overt about their willingness to compete: it's out in the open, well examined, and follows known rules. I have seen men in meetings behaving as if they were in a boxing match. They start, compete, and then, when the winner has been determined, they shake hands and move on, and might later go out together for a meal, with no residue of anger or ill will from the conflict.

Women compete covertly, pretending that it is not happening, all the while measuring themselves against their perceived rivals. We are stuck somewhere between wanting to please the "tribe," to feel accepted, and the urge to assert our own way and win. Our conflicts sometimes never manifest in the form of an outright argument, but can simmer under the surface for years.

I have observed two main issues in female competition. The first is internal insecurity. We tend to compare ourselves to other women and derive our feeling of self-worth (or the lack thereof) through slotting ourselves into a hierarchy relative to them. We are better or worse than they are, according to an arbitrary scale that we determine—or have internalized and now unwittingly perpetuate. The comparison could be about looks, age, intelligence, skills, resources, or choice of mate. The lower we feel, the stronger we compete.

The second is external insecurity. We all need to feel like we are safe in our environment. What is considered "safe" varies and is determined by a variety of factors, including previous experience, trauma, and habits. Some women have a strong need to control their environment, which can lead to competitiveness as a means of staying on top of whatever threat is perceived. This could be competition for a potential mate, financial security, or a high rank in the social order. Typically, the more secure we feel in ourselves and our surroundings, the less we feel the need to compete.

The answer to these issues is not just to play nice and get along. It is often suggested that if we remembered the ancient collaborative "sisterhood," we would not enter into competition. As I just illustrated, competition is needed for finding your place in the tribe, and serves our survival in both the ancient and modern sense.

If there is an answer, it is to remedy the feelings of low self-esteem and lack of external control. One way to do so is by engaging in community that self-regulates, supports, and strengthens each member as both an individual and as part of the tribe. Unfortunately, there are not many openly available gatherings that would qualify as such. Sororities, PTA, and charitable groups are notorious for their infighting and fierce competition.

However, there are longstanding women's groups in which these dynamics have been adequately explored, examined, and resolved. I have found that quilt circles, craft groups, and book clubs that are long established often are the most supportive and collaborative environments. The best groups I have experienced are comprised of a variety of ages and backgrounds.

I often get invited to speak at various women's groups, and am always surprised how willing the groups are to make new women feel welcome. If you are interested in connecting with other women in an informal way, visit a few groups until you feel a kinship and shared interest with one. Or you can start your own, as I did all those years ago. Conflict and competition will occur no matter what, but with mutual care and respect, these issues can be used to create a strong and lasting connection.

Sisterhood is not an assumed bond enforced through ideology. It is a living, breathing, always changing organism with its own innate genius. Gathering to allow a relaxed and undemanding space in which this genius can unfold is one way to address the challenges we face. The activity, however mundane, is just a portal through which we enter the deep magic of communion.

The activity itself also takes on a certain magic in this environment. Imagine the energy of food prepared in this context, or rugs woven, or a friend's new apartment or house painted and decorated.

Through being with other women, contributing and connecting, we get to see ourselves through their eyes. We learn self-esteem through their esteem for us. We learn from them as they benefit from our learning. Through our connection, we all become human. Our bodies learn from each other effortlessly when given the space to do so. We share stories, history, triumph, and pain. We discuss our insecurities and our goals, and as we do so, we keep each other in check and lift one another up.

Humans developed for thousands of years in tribal situations and not only survived but thrived as a species, evolving the ability and brain function to cooperate effectively on a local, tribal level as well as on a larger scale. Looking at this leads me to look at healthy communal self-regulation as a possible option for a more constructive and less stressful way for women to live in our current situation.

My life as it is would not be possible without the community of women around me. I am supported and in turn support several women with whom I have formed a close bond. Some of them I employ, some are neighbors and friends. The relationships we have are not free of conflict or misgivings, but we have deep respect for one another, and most importantly, we enjoy each other's company in an easy and nondemanding way. Sometimes just "hanging out" or sharing a glass of wine and a laugh at the end of the day is the medicine I need most.

....

My life as it is would not be possible without the community of women around me. I am supported and in turn support several women with whom I have formed a close bond.

....

In my Wild Woman's Circles, we explore these motifs in a more structured way, which I offer here as inspiration and a possible starting place for your own local group. At the beginning of each meeting, each woman shares about herself. I usually post a few guiding questions, such as, "What are you bringing to this group today?" "How are you today?" "How was your last month of practice?" "What would you like to have happen in the group today?"

The questions are just a starting point to bring everyone into the group. As each woman talks, we give her our undivided attention; only she is speaking, there are no comments made.

After the check-in, we engage in the various embodiment practices I outline throughout this book, and we use Non-Linear Movement® to sensitize our bodies. From there, we engage in themed explorations, perhaps around expression, or movement, or sharing of gifts. Each woman learns from the others and offers her own unique flavor. We end each group with a ritual. Sometimes we share chai or raw chocolate, sometimes we play with oracle cards, smudge and bless each other, or use essential oils for anointing and massaging each other.

Each group is different, but the elements are always the same:

Create connection and share with a check-in
Embodiment and sensitizing practices
Partnered exchanged through dance, performance, and talking
Ritual and closing

You can use all the practices described in this book, as I still do after all these years. By creating a structure and specific format, the group becomes a safe and relaxing container. We speak and share in a way that allows each woman to be heard. We practice the embodiment and sensitizing exercises shared with you in this book to encourage gentle and gradual re-wilding, and we use ritual as a means to connect us with one another and the divine.

As a leader of women's groups and as a woman in business, this is an ongoing exploration of mine, and an issue dear to my heart. I do believe that we need a community-based paradigm to truly thrive. Fostering women's community and connecting back to the tribe with the format described above, and using the exercises I am sharing with you in this book, are my offering at this time. My vision is to connect women to themselves and their bodies. As that gives us more capacity and availability toward others, it will open the door for deeper connection and collaboration.

15

Career

I LOVE MY WORK. EVERY ASPECT OF IT. I GET TO TRAVEL TO A VARIETY OF beautiful cities and retreat centers all over the world, where I am doing work that I find creatively inspiring. Even better, I get to do so with Steve James, my coteacher, who is not only a gifted human being and a close friend, but also inspires me and creates constant fresh direction for our business. We have wonderful longtime students and interesting participants on three continents. My work feels like an ongoing, exciting adventure.

In my private practice, I work with famous and talented performers, actors, and artists. I also consult in the field of high-performance business and second-generation wealth. This work brings me to movie sets, photo shoots, sold-out stadiums, and charity events. I have done sessions on private planes, yachts, islands, and in luxury hotels. My clients are incredible human beings and a joy to be around.

Pretty amazing, right? Yes, and I am incredibly grateful for my life! However, what I have not said yet is that this *is* my life. Every day. All day. There has not been a single day in the last twenty-plus years during which I am not deeply immersed in the management of this endeavor.

I have been self-employed ever since I started counseling, and found out quickly that managing, booking, and billing clients takes almost as much time as seeing clients. And when you spend eight hours a day in sessions, which is how I built my business to begin with, there is no space for any of the other logistics of life. All of that has to be handled before and after work hours, essentially adding another full-time job to my life.

When I started teaching, I quickly discovered that the logistics/marketing/venue booking/e-mail answering/traveling part of the business takes ten times as much work as the actual teaching. Factor in creation of new content, and jet lag, and you have an every-waking-hour situation.

This is all to say that I built an amazing career and have accomplished most of what I set out to do. I am still as inspired to teach, support, and share knowledge in the way that it was shared with me when I started out in life. However, my success required sacrifice. I built my business by investing all my time and energy into it, with very little attention to anything else. There were no vacations and no days off for the first ten years. I dated only casually during the time I was building my business from scratch. (I knew only one person when I moved to Los Angeles.)

One reason this was possible is that I didn't have children—not because I couldn't have them, but because I didn't get married until my late thirties, and ultimately decided not to have children, given the circumstances of my work life.

I am very happy with the choices I have made, but the point here is that I had to make choices. I could not have it all, even though I certainly tried. There are decisions that come with having a career, many of which are not apparent when we start out.

When I was scanning to make my selection of which related topics to focus on in this chapter, I found that each of them had a multitude of facets and related opinions, hotly discussed divergent ideas, and ideologies. I was struck by just how skewed, tainted, and dogmatically and ideologically influenced the reporting and research I found was. From the wage gap to gender equality—or the lack thereof—to messages around how to integrate children and work, I found it almost impossible to glean data that was not heavily influenced by agendas.

Recognizing this, I decided to write mostly about my own experiences and the results of my consulting work. My focus became to communicate what I deemed to be the most useful aspect I had to offer on each topic.

For myself, as a woman actively engaged in these considerations, as a professional with more than forty thousand hours of counseling under my belt, and as a workshop teacher traveling internationally, I have certainly found that no answer and solution fits all, or all the time. While there are general ideas that are useful to consider and that can guide our process, the magic comes from giving people the tools and space to feel and explore, whether that is through talking, somatic exploration, or relaxation. Decisions around dating, relationship, children, and career are nuanced and deserve well-informed and thoughtful consideration.

Once good information has been presented and the space and opportunity for exploration has been opened, decisions can be made from a more holistic place.

With that in mind, I am writing only about the topics here that are distinct to each woman's personal preferences and her individual situation.

Let's look at the term "career." The dictionary defines it as "an occupation undertaken for a significant period of a person's life and with opportunities for progress." A career means choosing a path of work that has meaning and a trajectory. A job pays a wage but might not be something that has advancement or progression. Perhaps in the course of career development, one takes a job, but that job would then fall into the category of time, money, and energy invested in pursuing an occupation.

Career and the topic of the next chapter—children—are inextricably connected for women. Even though we are more able than ever before to pursue careers in almost any chosen field, we are still the ones growing human beings within our bodies. We still give birth and, ideally, feed our babies with our bodies. And, human babies still require a lot more care, contact, and parenting than any other mammal. Raising children well is an incredibly demanding job of great responsibility.

Our advancement as women in the workplace and our freedom to choose what kind of life we want are directly tied to reproduction. Only since the invention of the birth control pill have women been able to choose when and how many children they wanted, and that choice has influenced what kind of work they can pursue. Access to reliable birth control is a key factor in choosing and maintaining a career.

....

> **Only since the invention of the birth control pill have women been able to choose when and how many children they wanted, and that choice has influenced what kind of work they can pursue.**

....

This is why many advocacy groups recommend the universal availability of funded birth control, particularly in low-income areas. The lower the socioeconomic status of a woman, the less choice there is to begin with. Often this means working two or more low-paying jobs to make ends meet. If access to low-cost birth control is unavailable to these women, their autonomy and freedom can be severely curtailed.

Only when we have decided if and when we want children can we look at how much time, energy, and money we want to invest into our careers.

There is also an issue my clients and students often speak about, which is a conundrum not easily addressed and often considered not directly correlated to career choice. If you want children, then logic implies that you probably would like to have a partner to conceive and raise your children with.

Very few women I have counseled want to pick a suitable father at a sperm bank and go through the whole process of conception, pregnancy, birth, and child-rearing alone—all while working full time to support themselves and their children. That is usually reserved for a different scenario, in which the woman can't find a partner or maintain a relationship, and reproductive time is running out. Often the women making this choice report having spent their essential fertile years pursuing careers and working, in some cases, up to eighty hours a week.

So, tracking back from there, how much time we want to invest in work during our fertile years is a consideration unique to women.

If training for a career and then pursuing that career keeps a woman, logistically speaking, from finding a mate, and she wants a relationship and possibly children, that's something to truthfully consider. This does not even take into account the fact that a high-stress, high-pressure work environment is not exactly conducive to feeling our bodies, or receptiveness to connecting with another, as we discussed in chapter 6: "Embodiment," pp. 71–81.

....

If training for a career and then pursuing that career keeps a woman, logistically speaking, from finding a mate, and she wants a relationship and possibly children, that's something to truthfully consider.

....

There are quite a few books in which it is suggested that we should have it all—that career and children can be reconciled, and that it is only a matter of sharing responsibility between the spouses, that we owe it to the "sisterhood" to claim our rightful place in the workforce.

I have several clients, all of them married to equally successful men, who come home from a full day of the high-stress work of running companies and then take turns saying "good night" to their children—the children with whom the nanny has spent the whole day, whom she has cared for, bathed, and put to bed. My clients report that they alternate nighttime "duty" with their husbands, and that on average the two of them spend maybe a combined total of one hour a day during the workweek interacting with their children. Not everyone wants to make that choice, and not everyone wants their children raised by a nanny so that they themselves can pursue a career.

I don't think that it is useful to accuse a woman of selling out women's liberation if she wants children and wants to raise them herself instead of becoming a CEO, nor do I think that we should look down on women who choose to prioritize career advancement over having children.

Dr. Jordan B. Peterson, professor of psychology at the University of Toronto, in a talk on gender equality, perhaps phrased the issue of women and career best: The question is not, "Why are there not more women in positions of power?" The question is, "Why are there any men insane enough ever to occupy these positions?"[12]

He speaks about the single-minded focus it takes to advance a career and how most women (and men, for that matter) don't want to work that many hours.

He further discusses quality of life as a big consideration for women. Pursuing one's chosen profession can take a lot of time and energy: first schooling and training, then breaking into the field, all while working a lot of hours. It is not uncommon for some women who work in the more competitive professions, like law, to be required to work sixty to eighty hours a week.

Dr. Peterson points out that women's self-reported happiness has gone down significantly over the last thirty years, mainly because of the heightened workload that comes from having children and jobs.[13]

British Author Fay Weldon, who wrote the second-wave feminist classic *The Life and Loves of a She-Devil*, echoes Dr. Peterson's thoughts on jobs versus career: "As soon as women have the choices of marrying or not marrying, having children, or not, the only choice they don't have is not earning, which is a terrible loss to womanhood."[14]

Both Dr. Peterson and Ms. Weldon each go on to speak about the fact that most people don't end up with a career, they end up with a job, which goes from nine to five and enables them to have a family, while a career might be 24/7/365.[15][16]

Dr. Peterson also discusses that above a certain income level, money can no longer be equated with well-being, and that time spent with a partner and children often becomes a higher priority than making money as we mature.[17]

The positive aspect of all this is the fact that we, for the most part, have the privilege to choose. Nevertheless, for the choice to be an actual thought-and-felt-through decision, we do need good information, well thought-out arguments for all options, and the space to decide, free of dogma and ideology.

No matter what you choose or what your orientation is, one thing I can say for sure, from my own experience, is this: Pursuing a career comes with sacrifice.

Regardless of how organized, resourced, and practiced we might be, there are only so many hours in the day. Time is the most valuable commodity and the only one we all have in equal amounts. How we choose to spend our time and how we prioritize time consumption is entirely up to us. The fact is, creating, maintaining, and furthering a career will use up many hours of the day. Some other areas will need to receive less time and attention. Those areas are the areas of sacrifice.

. . . .

Regardless of how organized, resourced, and practiced we might be, there are only so many hours in the day. Time is the most valuable commodity and the only one we all have in equal amounts.

. . . .

This is not necessarily an issue, as long as you know what you have chosen and what you are choosing to sacrifice.

Twelve hours at work are twelve hours that you don't spend with your intimate partner or on self-care. Assuming that you have seven hours of sleep at night and twelve hours of work, you will have only five waking hours left in your day. How you want to spend your precious life is really the bigger question here.

For me, personally, it is all totally worth it! I have made choices I am happy with, and even though sometimes I consider what my life would look like if I had taken a job or had children, I feel like I am spending my time well, in worthwhile, meaningful pursuits.

A big part of re-wilding yourself is the ability to honestly assess what you want and what you are capable of. When you are sensitive to the messages your body sends, you are able to assess your capabilities and heed your intuition. By including your body's signals in any decision-making process, you are caring for yourself in an authentic way. From there, the decisions around career take on a different perspective. As you come into your own and are able to use instinct, intuition, and power, your choices become increasingly free from peer pressure and societal expectations. You can choose what aligns with your true nature.

16

Children

THIS IS NOT A CHAPTER ABOUT CHILD-REARING OR HOW TO EQUIP YOUR children for life in these fast-paced times. I don't have children and am therefore not qualified to give any advice on those subjects.

I am, however, a passionate advocate for women choosing to be mothers, the operative word here being "choosing"—not from a place of having to fulfill your debt to society or your parents' wish for a grandchild—not because you have to, but because you yearn to, because you want to, because you desire to bring forth a valuable human being and equip him or her with the best you've got.

The choice to become a parent is, now more than ever, a complex one. There are considerations around career: who will be the primary caretaker and where the child will be when you are at work. There are financial considerations, since for many couples, both partners have to work to make a living. For single parents, this is also a big issue, with childcare and livelihood needing to be handled simultaneously.

Many women I have worked with ask themselves if it is right to bring a child into a world that's so uncertain; others feel guilty for wanting a baby when they have been told repeatedly that a career is what is ultimately empowering for a woman.

All human beings come from a mother. So far, there is no other way. Giving birth is the most ordinary and the most sacred thing. It's been done since the beginning of time and yet, every birth is a miracle.

....

All human beings come from a mother. So far, there is no other way. Giving birth is the most ordinary and the most sacred thing. It's been done since the beginning of time and yet, every birth is a miracle.

....

As a mother, you become a living sacrifice. Birth in itself is dangerous, even today (the US has 28 maternal deaths per 100,000 women—more than many developing countries), and women are built to give of themselves, literally giving of their bodies to their children, and putting the well-being of their children above their own.

I have been present at close to thirty births, some of them in hospitals, some at home, some traumatic, some ecstatic, each of them a pure and astounding miracle.

I cried at every single one of them, moved beyond words, regardless of the circumstances. There is the journey through pregnancy; the moment when the contractions start; the sometimes easeful, sometimes agonizing hours of labor; and the moment of transition when the baby needs to be pushed out; with everyone present having a single focus. This is a journey deeply natural to women and shared by all women who have given birth throughout all time, something profoundly expressive of our wild nature in ways that few experiences are. Birth is an initiation, an archetypal journey that still holds the potential for its counterpoint, death. Suddenly, there it is: new life where just a moment ago there was only a woman with a rather large belly!

It's touching to see new parents in whatever configuration they might be. Heterosexual couples, lesbian and gay couples, and single mothers all react with the same pure joy and awe. Those of you reading this who have children will remember your own story, and regardless of how the birth itself went, it ended with a child being placed into your hands and, with that, the care for this little human being began.

I am aware that not every birth results in a live baby, and not every child is wanted, and those circumstances are tragic and filled with grief. For the sake of this chapter I am focusing on the choice to have children and related considerations.

Long before your due date, the considerations around the "right" kind of pregnancy and birth start. Once again, our options and choices have vastly increased. Nowadays we can have everything from midwife-assisted home births to high-tech, scheduled C-sections.

And again, as it seems to be with most women's issues, the opinions and agendas around birth are strong. Even though I have strong opinions on this subject myself, the important issue here is proper education and information. How you want to birth your child is, in the end, up to you, and only you will be responsible for the outcomes of those decisions. Getting factual information and weighing all the options are key here.

Age, health status, risk factors, environment, financial considerations, lifestyle, and parenting goals all factor into the decisions around pregnancy and birth. So do religious and cultural conditioning.

My advice here is to talk to many women who have given birth and ask about their experiences. Ask women who have had all different kind of births, inform yourself of your options, tour hospitals and birthing centers, and speak with women who had successful home births, as well as those who did not. Birthing groups and internet forums are good resources. As always, you will have to separate the wheat from the chaff and sense what is right for you.

> Ask women who have had all different kind of births,
> inform yourself of your options, tour hospitals and
> birthing centers, and speak with women who had
> successful home births, as well as those who did not.

And while you are at it, inform yourself about yet another hotly discussed topic: breastfeeding. Ideally, you will be well aware of its benefits and potential difficulties, and have options for support with it long before giving birth.

Often, despite the best-laid plans, the birth turns out different from what you planned; a friend of mine who wanted a hospital birth gave birth at home on her bathroom floor, alone, in the middle of a massive blizzard. Whatever the birth circumstances turn out to be, preparation is key, and knowledge is definitely power.

Children bring great joy and great responsibility. In my many years of private practice, I have seen every parenting style and challenge imaginable.

Two of the main issues clients come to me with are: suddenly diminished or absent sexual intimacy; and the realization that they had unrealistic ideas and expectations around having children.

When it comes to new parenthood, I often tell my clients to place no expectations on themselves to be sexy lovers and sensual creatures for a while. Giving birth and healing from it is demanding. Breastfeeding, caring for an infant, waking up at night and adjusting to being a parent can be all-consuming. These precious stages are to be savored, and it's important to give this natural process the time it needs to fully unfold.

Add to this the day-to-day demands of life and you'll have more than enough to do. This is not to say that you can't have beautiful intimacy and deep sexual experiences (with yourself or a partner), but as always, pressure and striving are antidotes to such experiences. Give yourself time and space to let this experience unfold.

There is no need to buy into the motherhood edition of the Super-woman Syndrome!

You don't need to be in perfect shape a month after birth. There is no need to have your child sleep through the night immediately. You will be tired and achy. You most likely won't turn back into a ravenous sex goddess as soon as you are healed. And no, motherhood is not purely instinctual; some things you'll have to be taught (this is what support and your tribe is for), and that does not make you a bad mother!

If you are currently deciding whether or not to have children, I would suggest you make a list about all the reasons why you want to have and raise children. Be specific and, most importantly, be honest.

Before you speak with others about it, become clear about your motivations and expectations. Sure, there is always an X factor involved, as you won't really know for sure how you'll feel until you have experienced it. And maybe, to you, having children is just what one does inevitably with one's life. However, examining your hopes and motivations honestly can enable you to make the best decisions and choices possible and get the support you need along the way.

Expressing one's true nature is not always convenient or easy. How and if you want to be a mother is, more than ever, a deeply individual decision as the pressures of society and convention lessen. The Wild Women I personally have seen through this process shared one common trait: they spent time exploring who they were before having children, explored their desires, and fostered a sensual and caring relationship with themselves.

The stronger and more fulfilled you are before becoming a parent, the better you will be able to raise and love another human being.

IV

Sacred Practices of the Wild Woman

A Note on Practice

THE FOLLOWING PRACTICES ARE MEANT TO INSPIRE AND RECONNECT you to your body, nature, and the beauty within and around you. Rather than approaching them as yet another chore or obligation, you can take them as an invitation to return to your natural flow.

All the practices are designed to be small reminders and motivations, and each can be done in as little as five minutes, so as not to add any additional load to your busy day. When you have more time, you can expand any of these for as long as you want, but I would recommend starting out with less than you think you can do.

Create New Habits

We are creatures of habit. As I noted in earlier chapters, whatever we repeat most becomes our predominant pattern. For integrated education, it is best for us to combine three aspects of our being: cognitive understanding, which gives us an intellectual underpinning; emotional resonance, which helps us acknowledge and integrate our feelings; and somatic learning, which connects us to our body's innate wisdom and creates permanent change. Therefore, these practices speak to our minds, our feelings, and our bodies.

These practices train your body to soften, relax, and reconnect to its innate wisdom. Whatever activities you perform most in daily life shape your habits and dispositions. Most of us spend the majority of our time in directed, hurried, and stressful activities. All the practices given here are designed specifically to counteract these tendencies and give you easy access to your feminine nature.

Little and Often

To establish new habits, doing these practices for a few minutes at a time, and repeating them often, gives greater benefit than doing one long weekend session. Even if you move your body only to one song a day, or simply light a candle at your desk as you start work, the accumulation of these practices will, over time, shift your perception and attitude.

Set a Time

With all practices, it is best to determine how much time you will spend on each session beforehand, and set a timer. You can always go longer if you have the time and energy, but try not to cut short the duration you chose. It is important for practices to have a formal beginning and end, as this creates clarity and relaxation in the body. You can even bow to yourself, or offer any other gesture you like, in order to formally end the practice before you transition into whatever is next.

Do Only What Speaks to You

Most important is to look at these practices as a treat and not a chore. Pick only what speaks to you and what you genuinely want to do. Don't be aspirational. Be realistic, and be kind to yourself. It is much better to pick one thing to practice and stick with it for a month than it is to make big plans and then get waylaid by stress two days after starting, and then get upset with yourself for not following through.

Explore for Yourself

The practices in this book are meant as explorations, not prescriptions. By doing them, you will find out about yourself. Many of them are purposely designed to give you access to your inner workings. Instead of telling you how you will feel when you are doing them, I invite you to investigate them, and explore, as you practice, how you are really feeling and what habit patterns and considerations show up.

For instance, you might expect that the dance practice will leave you feeling elated and happy, but maybe when you move your body to one particular song, other kinds of feelings show up. Maybe you can feel your resistance to moving, or your block to taking time for yourself. Perhaps you feel awkward in your body, or maybe doing unstructured movement releases pent-up feelings. By engaging in these simple practices, you get to feel what is really present for you, instead of layering the expectation of a possible outcome over the experience.

1. The Wild Woman's Foundational Practice

If you have time for only one practice, I would suggest you do the practice that any woman I teach personally starts out with. This potent, foundational practice is called "Moving What You Are Feeling," and touches on many principles at once. It supports embodiment, releases stuck energy, sensitizes you to your feelings and sensations, brings your emotions to "current," and increases sensual awareness.

You can do just one song a day, and expand from there whenever you have time or energy to do so.

Moving What You Are Feeling

Put on a piece of music. Ideally, as mentioned before, pick a piece that has a good beat, with no lyrics. Begin by just standing. Feel your feet on the ground and mentally give yourself this time for yourself.

Begin moving your body with whatever you are feeling. If you feel stress, move as stress. If you feel numb, move as numbness. This is not a dance, and there is absolutely no need to look good, or even feel good. This is an exploration into how your body wants to move when given permission to do so. You'll notice that, as you move, the next sensation will arise, and you will begin moving with that sensation or feeling.

Don't follow the impulse to use structured dance moves; don't even attempt to move with the rhythm. Just let whatever your body feels be translated into motion. Sounds might happen, emotions will come and go; perhaps you will feel nothing, which is also fine, just keep on moving with whatever shows up. You can set a specific time to practice this, for as short as one song, and as long as you wish. It's important, though, to decide on a specific time beforehand and stick with it for the duration. Set a timer or create a playlist of desired length.

2. Embodiment and Aliveness

Feeling and expressing through our bodies is the source of pleasure, power, and deep bodily wisdom. Connection and aliveness in your body allows for the full experience and articulation of who we are. Let your glorious feminine nature unfold through these simple yet potent practices!

Move to a Song Each Day

Pick a song that represents your current mood or taste. Find a place where you can move your body undisturbed for the duration of the song. Let yourself dance with abandon, bringing attention to the movement of your feet, thighs, and pelvis. Notice whatever feelings arise as you move, and don't try to alter your experience. The main purpose of this exercise is to feel your body move and bring the energy from the head and shoulders down into the rest of your body.

Hip Circles

Stand barefoot with your feet hip-width apart. Bring your hands onto your hips and begin to make circles with your hips. Start out with small, subtle motions and widen the motion only as your hips awaken to the movement. The key here is not to force your body to open faster than it wants to. Particularly since we sit for long periods of time, it is important not to "wrench" the hips open. As your hips awaken, you can experiment with different motions.

Try going faster or slower than you normally would. Move your hips in figure eights, and if you feel like having fun, try writing your name with your hip movements. Make sure your feet are solidly planted on the ground. When you are ready to finish, make the movements gradually subtler until you come to complete stillness. Stand with your eyes closed and feel all the different sensations within your body.

Bouncing

Stand barefoot with your feet a bit wider than hip-width. Take a moment and feel where your feet connect with the ground. Bring attention to the soles of your feet and your ankles, and feel your calves. Your upper body is relaxed and upright, with your arms just hanging by your sides. Begin bouncing up and down by bending and straightening your knees, without locking them on the way up.

As you bounce, keep your feet firmly planted on the ground. Let your whole upper body and head follow along. See if you can feel the whole front surface of your body beginning to relax as you imagine the tension in your body is bounced downward, and drops out the base of the body. Allow your shoulders to bounce and relax. You can even relax your jaw and let your mouth loosen with each bounce.

Try bouncing fast, then slow, then finding a rhythm you can keep for the duration of your practice. Feel your thighs becoming activated and, when they do, relax the tension instead of bracing against the sensation. Allow your breathing to be natural so it can change as your body adjusts to the motion. When you are ready to finish, make the movements more and more subtle until you come to complete stillness. Stand with your eyes closed and feel all the different sensations within your body.

Foot Massage

Gather your favorite body cream or oil and a towel, and find a position in which you can reach your own feet comfortably.

Starting with one foot, apply some rich cream and massage, with varying pressure, the whole sole of your foot. Pay particular attention to the instep and the very center of the foot. Then massage each toe, giving it a light tug. Next, lightly massage the top of your foot, tracing the lines from between your toes to your ankle. Massage around your ankle, then move to the Achilles tendon and massage behind each ankle. When you encounter an area of tension or tenderness, spend some extra time on those spots. Make sure not to press too hard on an area of soreness, instead applying consistent medium pressure, coaxing instead of forcing the area into relaxing. Proceed the same way with the other foot. Make sure to wipe the bottom of your feet with a towel before you get up so you don't slip or stain the floor. Once you are standing, feel your feet and the way they connect with the ground underneath you. In the Tantric traditions, this is considered a way to connect oneself to the earth through the body and bring the energy down from the head. If you want to, you can praise your body and feet as you touch each part.

3. Relaxation

A relaxed body is a feeling body. Relaxation is the source of sensitivity, pleasure, and intuition. It allows for your power to be channeled and fully used, instead of being bound up in excess tension and effort. Relaxing your body calms your mind and allows your emotions to flow freely. Enjoy these practices! They are not an indulgence, but an essential tool for your well-being.

Take a Relaxing Bath

Make sure that you have at least thirty minutes for yourself. Draw yourself a bath and add magnesium bath flakes. (Soaking in transdermal magnesium is one of the best ways to relax muscles and replenish.) Bring in all the special touches that you enjoy—perhaps light some candles or add a few drops of essential oil to your water; pour yourself a drink, or make a cup of tea; play some music or read your favorite book. Use lavender for relaxation, eucalyptus for easy breathing, ylang-ylang for sensuality, or rose for inviting love. Make sure the water is not too hot so you can immerse for fifteen to twenty minutes and let your body and muscles relax. This is a great way to transition from the day into bedtime. The magnesium relaxes the muscles, and the subsequent cooling down of your body induces sleep. (Make sure not to use phones, computers, or any kind of electronic screen after bath and before bed, as the light emitted from them will reactivate wakefulness.)

Energetic Cleanse at the End of Your Shower

Take a moment in the shower to let the water stream directly on your forehead. Stand under the stream and let the water run over your head and the front of your body. (Make sure the water is not too hot.) As the water massages your forehead, imagine that all tension runs off your body and down the drain. If you feel adventurous, end with a cold water burst, for added vitality.

Self-Massage

After your bath or shower, spread a cozy towel onto the floor that is large enough for you to sit on comfortably. Pat yourself dry, but leave some water on your skin. Lightly massage some almond or sesame oil onto your damp skin, starting with the feet and moving over the calves, knees, and upward toward the thighs. Using circular motions from right (upward) to left (downward), massage the belly and make your way upward—over the breasts and all the way to the neck. Massage each hand, forearm, and upper arm, and then the shoulders and neck. Gently wipe your feet, so you don't slip or stain the floor, and then slowly stand, massaging the buttocks and as much of your back as you can reach. To end your massage, apply moisturizer to your face in an upward, circular motion, and use your fingertips to massage your scalp and ears. A self-massage is an excellent time to bring focus to caring for yourself. Say a few words of appreciation to yourself about each body part as you touch it. Speak to yourself as a loving friend or as a lover would speak to you about your body. Slather yourself in praise, no matter how odd it might feel. Over time, your words will sink into your being, and your relationship to your body will deepen.

Restorative Pose against a Sofa or Wall

Find a place to lie down and elevate your feet. This could be with your calves resting on a sofa (make sure your calves and thighs are at a right angle to each other) or with your calves and thighs against the wall. If you are elevating against a wall, the trick is to lie on your side, and scoot your butt as close to the wall as possible, with your legs on the floor against the wall. From there, pivot onto your back and lean the entire length of your legs against the wall. Let your arms rest by your sides and close your eyes. For added relaxation, place an eye pillow over your eyes. Set the timer for a minimum of five minutes. When you are done, roll onto your side and lie there for a moment, feeling your body and transitioning into whatever you do next.

Lower Body Relaxation

For a moment, turn your attention to the hips, pelvic area, and buttocks. If you are seated, feel where your body meets the chair. Notice the quality of muscular activity. Are your buttocks clenched? Do you have tension in your pelvic floor? Can you feel sensations in your genitals? Is your energy pulled up and in?

Without changing anything, take a snapshot of the muscular tension and any feeling that comes with it. Identify the area with the most tension, and slowly, start tensing that area even more. (You might be able to isolate the muscles or you might just tighten the whole pelvic region a bit more.) Squeeze and tighten as you inhale for a moment, then exhale and let go of tension as much as you can.

Notice the sensations as you relax. Based on what you observe, begin to bring your attention toward relaxing the lower body. Once again, you can do this nearly anytime, anywhere.

4. Re-sensitizing

Many of us have diminished or "turned off" our subtle sensation, as a reaction to stress or trauma, or as a means of protecting ourselves from the sensory and information overload of our daily lives. These practices invite you back to listening and feeling deeply within. They engage and open the natural intelligence of your being, and awaken your innate wisdom.

Very Subtle Touch—Sexual and Nonsexual

This practice can be done with any part of your body. An easy way to begin is by using your dominant hand to touch your nondominant hand. Touch the top of your hand with one finger, very lightly. Observe the sensations that arise as you run your finger over your hand. Experiment with different motions, speeds, and with more and less pressure. See how light and subtle you can make the touch and still perceive pleasant sensations. This same exploration can also be used during self-pleasure, as a way to re-sensitize areas that are used to high stimulus (such as strong vibrators or hard touch).

Cat/Cow

Find an area where you can kneel comfortably. A bit of padding is recommended. Come onto your hands and knees and drop your head so your neck relaxes. Position your hands and knees so that you feel stable and supported. (If you have weak wrists, you can come down onto your forearms.) Take a moment to notice your breath, but don't change anything. Just let the breath be and begin following its natural rhythm with your motions. As you inhale, drop your belly toward the ground, making more space for the inhalation (this is called the "cow" position in yoga), then, when your inhalation comes to an end, begin arching your back upward into the "cat" position as you exhale. This position naturally squeezes out the breath. Once you begin inhaling again, drop the belly again, and so on. The important part of this exploration is that you follow the breath with your movements instead of conforming your breath to the even rhythm of the movement. Our natural breath is designed to adapt to the body's oxygen requirements, and if not imposed upon, will change based on metabolic need. Following your breath will sensitize you to the needs and signals of your body. This is one of the most effective sensitizing practices I know, and has the additional health benefits of enlivening your spinal muscles after long sitting, moving your lymph, and increasing circulation.

Decreasing External Input

As I've mentioned, overwhelm and excess stimulation numb us to the signals of our body. As an experiment, reduce input for a few hours, days, or weeks. Identify a potential source of excess input—such as TV, internet, or social media—and eliminate or reduce it. This could be as simple as not watching, listening to, browsing, or reading any media, and not texting or calling anyone during one part of your day. Notice what arises when the "noise" is reduced, and let yourself feel those sensations, avoiding the temptation to try to drown them out with more activity.

Sitting Practice

Find a comfortable position, either on a cushion or a chair. It is more important that the position allows you to sit still with minimum discomfort for the duration than that it looks good. Set a timer for ten minutes, and sit still for that time. You can have your eyes open or closed, whichever you prefer. There is no need to direct your thoughts or breath; simply sit and do absolutely nothing. Notice what arises for the duration. As you complete the practice, make sure to stand up carefully, mindful of your knees, especially if you are sitting on the ground.

5. Movement

I can't say enough about moving your body as a feminine practice! Regardless of the modality, setting your body into motion has incredible benefits. Now more than ever, since most of us spend so much time sitting, movement is probably the most important practice. Our bodies were designed to move, roam, hunt, gather, and do physical work. When the body does not move enough, we get stuck, not only physically, but also emotionally and mentally.

Have you ever noticed that you felt much clearer after a walk or workout? One of my great passions is guiding clients to experience somatic therapies and movements. Our emotions and thoughts and our bodies are intricately interconnected, and often the best way to tackle a life issue is through the body. The body remembers everything, and the body never lies. By engaging in movement, we allow the body's natural intelligence to be activated.

The Non-Linear Movement Method® (NLMM)

Over the years of seeing private clients, I often struggled with leaving my clients' problems, traumas, and emotions behind once the workday was over. This is a challenge well known to many care professionals.

While sitting across from eight clients a day, I would accumulate a fair share of heavy information and emotions. I often would lie in bed at night feeling numb or heavy with sadness and upset.

In the early days of my tantric training, I had learned to use motion instead of intellectual reasoning to let go of stuck energies. Instead of processing mentally what I felt in any given situation, I trained to be physically responsive. For example, when I had an upsetting conversation, I would allow myself to feel the anger or upset all throughout my body, instead of clenching down on the unpleasant sensation. This did not mean I would show the upset, necessarily; rather it meant that I allowed my body to feel and move with those sensations. It's an internal turning toward, rather than turning away from. Then, when I was able to work with my body, I would move my body and shake out any stuck feelings. Sometimes this would take a few minutes and result in some emotional release; sometimes it would take a few times until it felt like there was no more residue. A good way to tell if it was done was the absence of a mental loop about the event.

Over the years, I would use those practices as a way to get my body to release the aftereffects of acute stress situations that arose during sessions.

I began to experiment with the movement practices before I went to bed. Often, I was so tired that I would just get on my hands and knees right there on my bed. As I moved, I gained access to the emotions underneath the numbness, and my body and emotions would let go of the stressful events of the day.

Eventually I started using this modality with my clients as a way to get them unstuck and connected to their feelings during difficult sessions. Once I started teaching, this method became part of every workshop as a potent tool.

Now I find this method instrumental as a way to gently reintroduce women to their bodies in my workshops, and to help them restore their wild, embodied nature!

I have now practiced with this modality for more than thirty years, creating and refining this simple movement as a method that can be applied and taught effectively.

In recent years, my teaching partner, Steve James, has helped to clarify the method and its specific uses, and now we teach it as a powerful somatic modality. As described in earlier chapters, we call it the Non-Linear Movement Method® (NLMM.) Here are a few uses of NLMM:

Smoothes Out the Nervous System

The demands of modern life create an overactive mind, and stress and tension in the body. NLMM encourages identifying and unwinding patterns of contraction, and, through gentle, non-forced movements, relieves bodily tension and underlying mental loops. The result is a systematic, self-guided unburdening of the nervous system.

Processes and Identifies Emotions

As the body unwinds and the mind relaxes its pressured pace, the emotions associated with these patterns become apparent and are let go. You can note recurring emotional loops for further processing, and at the same time allow emotions to simply rise and release.

Awakens Sexual Energy and Sensual Sensation

As tension, contraction, and emotion are being released, the body becomes sensitized and we are able to feel more deeply. One of the marked results of this sensitization is an ability to feel increased pleasure and well-being. Participants report an increased ability to connect through their bodies, both with themselves and others.

Releases Trauma Patterns into Flow

One of the results of traumatic experiences (fresh and old alike) is "freeze," in which body, mind, and emotions are stuck in a state of numbness. Often "freeze" is mistakenly perceived as a feeling of "calm/nothing," which results in an inability to release the experience and ease the bodily patterns. The NLMM facilitates continued movement, which gently opens the freeze pattern and allows for recognition and release of the underlying bodily and emotional patterns.

Unites Body and Mind Via Intimacy with Physical Sensation
Through continued engagement with contraction and release, and facilitation of emotional awareness, the ingrained patterns become apparent and less pronounced. Over time, physical sensation can be engaged with, and the acceptance and tolerance of all sensation increases. Intimacy with whatever is present is possible.

Creates High Bodily Responsiveness
NLMM educates the body to release and process contraction, stress, and emotional tension. The body becomes highly attuned to all sensations and can note, react to, or release those sensations fluidly and without having to attend to traumatic or suppressed backlog.

Opens Access to Bodily Wisdom
By putting the emphasis on movement and circumventing the analytical mind and loops of tense thinking, the natural intelligence of our bodies is accessed. Through gentle guidance, the mechanisms of "freeze" and refusal to feel are loosened, and bodily wisdom can create the necessary actions, responses, and releases.

Begin your Non-Linear Movement Method® Practice:

On a mat, come onto your hands and knees. Drop your head and feel where your body meets the ground for a moment. Let your neck relax, and feel your head hanging heavily, like a bowling ball. Close your eyes and begin to feel how your body wants to move. Perhaps you feel some tightness that you want to attend to; perhaps there is an area you'd like to stretch. There might be thoughts and emotions that arise as you begin to move. No matter what occurs, just continue to move your body in whatever ways it wants to move. Make sure not to apply any breathing techniques and also to allow the movements to be nonlinear, instead of reverting to postures you know from yoga or other exercises. Just allow yourself to feel and move, to move and feel. Allow whatever thoughts occur to rise and fall naturally. There is no right or wrong way to do this exercise; simply allow your body to move and your body's natural wisdom to guide you.

Sometimes you'll be lost in thoughts; sometimes you might feel enveloped in emotions; sometimes you might just feel bored—all of which is fine—just continue moving.

You can do this movement with music as a background or in silence. The only two rules are: keep your eyes closed and keep moving, even if you are just moving a little finger or a making a slight undulation of the spine. You can also adjust your posture or position according to your body's needs, by lying down or resting on your forearms instead of putting pressure on your wrists. This exercise is best done on hands and knees, though, as this position gives you maximum movement of the spine, shoulders, and neck.

The key in NLMM is that it "unfreezes" you, and with that, the body's natural genius can release and attend to whatever needs to be let go. As I described in chapter 6: "Embodiment" and chapter 7: "Barriers to Embodiment," stress, tension, overwhelm, and trauma of all kinds tend to put us into fight, flight, or freeze mode.

Of those three responses, freeze is the hardest to detect and work with, as you are frozen, which creates a numbness that makes you "feel fine." With this gentle non-force method, stored tension and emotion as well as programmed coping patterns can be loosened; and as the body moves it can facilitate its own release and restoration. This exercise is a good entry into the method. It is simple and effective, and allows you to choose for yourself how much time you need.

Shake It Up! Nonhabitual Movement

Put on a piece of music and move your body however you want to move it. Notice the texture of your movement and the habitual ways your body expresses when you move to music. You might find that you use your arms and hands a lot, or that you lead mostly with your hips, or maybe you tend toward undulating motions, or slow motions. When you have discovered some of the key features of your usual movements, do the opposite. Shake it up and move in nonhabitual ways. Go slowly if you tend to go fast, make jagged motions if you tend toward smooth circles. Go against the rhythm and feel what that does to your body. The more you can interrupt your habits, the better!

Subtle Movement, Close to the Wall

Find a wall that you can lean against with your whole body. Press the front of your body against the wall, in whatever way feels good to you—perhaps pressing the side of your face onto the wall's cool surface, perhaps leaning your forehead against it. Close your eyes and begin to press different parts of your body against the wall through subtle motions. Take your time and feel each part you are pressing, and the subsequent set of emotions. Allow your feelings to rise, whatever they are, without holding on to them or trying to make them go away. Simply move, press, feel, and move again. You can put music on for this process, and you can also do this on a mat against the floor.

6. Expanding Your Repertoire

We each have our own specific flavor of the feminine. No two women are alike. As we relax into our natural flow, who we are as a flavor unfolds and infuses our actions and our life. A flavor is a bit like a unique combination of spices. Some women feel cool and soothing, some women are hot and spicy.

You can look at flavors as expressions of nature or as archetypes. They present themselves on a scale from light to dark. Here are a few examples:

Nature flavors could include: "Morning Dew," "The Ocean," "Thunderstorm and Lightning," and "Tornado."

Archetypal flavors could include: "Erotic Innocence," "Cheerleader," "Queen," "Femme Fatale," and "Dominatrix."

We naturally resonate with some of these flavors, and we are intimidated or repelled by others. For the sake of full feminine embodiment, it is interesting to expand your repertoire of feminine flavor expressions—not because who you are is "not good enough," but because, "Why not?"

You would not want just one pair, or one color of shoes, would you? Having an embodied repertoire of expression adds fun and range to who you are. It also infuses a different flavor into sexual intimacy and play.

Pick a Flavor and "Move" It

Pick a flavor and feel what this flavor feels like in your body. Put on a piece of music and move as this flavor. (You can use the same instructions given for "moving what you are feeling" here.) Let yourself "act out" this flavor. In the beginning, it will feel exactly like acting: your "flavor muscles" are not developed yet and it will feel strange, fake, and clumsy. Continue moving as this flavor, noticing what your body does in response. This is very much like a new workout; over time, you become more fluent in expressing a different part of you.

Imitate a Flavor—Learning through Resonance

Consider which actress or character fascinates you. This ideally pertains to a flavor you enjoy or admire. Perhaps you love the courage of Wonder

Woman, or the fiery nature of Penélope Cruz in *Vicky Cristina Barcelona*. Find a video clip of a scene you enjoy, and look at it repeatedly. Pay attention to how your body feels while watching it. Women learn through resonance, so just watching another woman move and speak is highly instructional. Allow yourself to feel the textures in your body, study the movements, mannerisms, and moods. You can also move your body, feeling how this character would move.

Each woman has a texture and, with a bit of practice, we can not only distinguish these textures, but also try them on to expand our own repertoire. For a moment, feel Penélope Cruz, and consider the following: Does her energy feel fiery, or cool and soothing? Is she relaxed or energetic? Are her movements undulating or sharp? Does she speak fast or slowly? Then, think of Grace Kelly. Is she soothing or fiery? How is her energy? How are her movements? Feel her tone and compare it to that of Penélope Cruz.

You can easily detect the difference in texture. You can do this same exercise with yourself, or even better, have a few friends do it together. Imitating textures that are different from your own is fun and allows you to have a fuller expression.

Play Dress-Up

For a fun, collaborative exploration on flavors, team up with a friend. Have your friend dress you up in clothes you would never choose yourself. These could be clothes from her closet, thrift store finds, or clothes you bought but are not wearing because they are "not you." Put on a different kind of makeup and alter your hairstyle so you look different from your usual appearance. The goal is to explore a different expression, not to look strange or hideous. You can do the same for your friend, then go out together and note if you are moving, acting, and speaking differently. Compare notes on how it feels and what you can each perceive.

These exercises are a great way to play with your friends or in a woman's group. Each woman will add her own flavor to the exploration.

7. Rituals

Rituals are as ancient as humanity itself. They anchor us, open us to the subtle realms, and remind us of what we are dedicated and devoted to. By using ritual, we create space, meaning, and purpose. By taking time away from our day-to-day lives, connecting with ourselves, beauty, and the senses, we enter a space of wider perception.

You can use your rituals to connect with your body, activating the deep knowing and wisdom available to you. Create your rituals in a way that is meaningful to you, but make sure to be formal and precise so they become ingrained in your being. Over time, you'll become more familiar with the specific steps, and the repetition of a specific ritual will allow you to enter the altered state of the particular occasion at hand. That's when the ritual develops its own magic.

The rituals described here can be done in a way that is very elaborate, or they can be shortened if you only have a brief moment to do them. You can enjoy them alone or together with friends.

Tea

Set time aside to create a pleasing setting to have a cup of tea. Set up an area with a nice cloth, teacup, and any other ingredients you'd like with your tea. I like to light a candle and include a small vase with a flower and arrange it in a way that gives me joy. Some of my favorite teas are Zhena's Gypsy Tea (raspberry Earl Gray), fresh Moroccan mint tea, and old-fashioned Yorkshire Gold. Take some time and explore different teas for different occasions. You could even invite friends for a tea-tasting party. Sometimes I'll have a cookie or a chocolate on a small saucer to enjoy with my tea. Make your tea in a pot and set it next to your cup.

If you enjoy music, put some music on and sit down. Light the candle, pour yourself some tea, and sit quietly for a moment enjoying the display before you. Then, as you sip your tea, bring your attention to the steam coming off the cup, inhale the fragrance of your tea before you drink, and savor the first sip. See if you can keep your attention on your sensory awareness: feeling the texture of the cup; listening to the sounds inside and outside the room; tasting the tea; smelling the tea, the flowers, and the candle; savoring any food you brought along. Relax the need to do anything else for this moment, knowing that you will reenter the demands of life in a short time. As you drink the tea, notice if any part of you is tense, impatient, or habitually "on alert" and let those feelings just be there without having to act on them or dissolve them. When you are done with your ritual, take the time to end it formally before you get up. A strong beginning and ending is important for any time away from your usual daily routine or activities.

If this takes too much logistical effort or time, you can always just make yourself a cup of tea and sit quietly, without distracting yourself, for however long the cup lasts, and enjoy your sensory perceptions.

Anointing

Pick out a few high-quality essential oils and a small bottle of almond oil from a health food store. There are many wonderful blends, both soothing and invigorating. Line up the essential oils and smell them one at a time; pick the one that speaks most to you in the moment. Put a few drops into your palm and rub your palms together to release the scent. Cup your palms in front of your nose, close your eyes, and inhale and enjoy the effects of the fragrance. Put a few drops of the almond oil into your palm, and add another few drops of the essential oil to it. Depending on your preferences, you can rub the mixture into your temples, onto your neck and chest, or massage your hands with it. Enjoy the stimulation of your senses and when you finish, make sure that you wipe your hands so as not to stain clothes and fabrics.

Oracle Cards

Find a set of tarot or oracle cards you enjoy visually. I have a large selection so I can choose according to my current mood. Create a space where you can lay out a few cards. Perhaps set the area with a beautiful cloth and a candle, then pour yourself a cup of tea and decide on a set time to spend engaged with the cards. There are a few options as to how.

You can just follow the procedure and protocol described in the instructions for the cards of your choice, or even do a full reading as described for the set. Or, you can use the artwork and words on the cards more like a visual meditation. You can ask a question as you pick the cards, state an intention, or just empty your mind. Pick one or three cards and arrange them on the cloth with the faces down. Then turn over one card at a time and look at it. Let the artwork inform your senses, and feel what each card invokes. Instead of reading the meaning of the card, just allow yourself to feel what the card does for you. Repeat this with each card, then sit back and allow yourself to just take in the colors, images, and artwork of the cards the same way you would look at a beautiful painting or photo. If you feel moved to do so, you can free-form journal about whatever the cards evoked. End the ritual by putting the cards back and freshly shuffling them before you close the box. As always, end the ritual with a gesture or a bow to close the occasion.

Smudging

The burning of incense, sage, resin, or wood is one of the oldest rituals in all traditions. The smoke produced is meant to clear the air, the space, and the energies around a person. Regardless of your personal beliefs, smudging is a good ritual to reset yourself and interrupt set patterns. Nowadays, you can buy many different kinds to suit your needs and preferences. Here are some of my favorites:

- Palo Santo: This is a fragrant wooden stick that, when lit, produces sweet, wood-smelling smoke.
- Sage: Smudge bundles of sage are easy to find and are commonly used to clear spaces.
- Sweetgrass: It is often sold as a braid for smudging, and also used as a medicinal herb.
- Incense sticks: There are many varieties and flavors. It's fun to try

different varieties until you find a few that you genuinely enjoy. Sticks are convenient, as they can be put on a holder while they continue burning once lit.

• Frankincense and copal: These are tree resins that need to be burned on a coal tablet or hot coal to release their distinct smells.

Regardless of which smudging material you choose, you can light it and then smudge either your body or the space you are in, or both. To smudge your body, move the smoke around every part of your body, including the bottom of your feet and the top of your head. Imagine that as the smoke surrounds you, everything in your body, your energy fields, and your life gets cleansed and renewed. You can add your own affirmation to your smudging if you choose, or use my favorite Native American smudging prayer:

> *May your hands be cleansed,*
> *that they create beautiful things.*
> *May your feet be cleansed,*
> *that they might take you where you most need to be.*
> *May your heart be cleansed,*
> *that you might hear its message clearly.*
> *May your throat be cleansed,*
> *that you may speak right when words are needed.*
> *May your eyes be cleansed,*
> *that you may see the signs and the wonders of the world.*
> *May this person and space be washed clean by the smoke, and may the*
> *same smoke carry our prayers.*[18]

To smudge a space, walk around each room and make sure that all corners have been smudged. You can put extra attention on all windows and doors and speak affirmations to clean your environment. When you are done, make sure that the smudging material is completely extinguished and that there is no chance of anything relighting or catching fire. (I almost burnt a house down once with a reignited sage bundle!)

Flower Arranging

Gather a few flowers on a walk, buy them, or pick them from your yard if you are lucky enough to have one. Find a glass or vase that can hold them. Handle each flower, appreciate its beauty, smell and touch it, and gently cut the stem at an angle. Then arrange the flowers in any way that is pleasing to you. You don't need to be a master florist or a Japanese Zen gardener; just follow your instincts and enjoy the interaction with each flower's texture and color. Place the arrangement so you can see it often and enjoy it throughout your day. I grow vast quantities of marigolds, which I love for their color, scent, and medicinal properties; I place them in small vases throughout my kitchen and office. Their color gives me such joy and reminds me of what's important to me. Sometimes, when I have time at home, I make garlands of marigolds to hang over pictures and statues in my studio.

Reading a Poem or Quote

I really did not like poetry until my mid-thirties, and I am still on the fence about certain kinds. I have gained an appreciation for the evocative nature of poetry, though, especially love poems and the ecstatic praises of mystics in all traditions.

Reading poetry to me is like tasting a good piece of chocolate or a small delicacy. There is a distinct taste to the poem; it evokes certain feelings, which can be revisited anytime by reading it again. Good poetry is like good music, you can read it over and over and enjoy it fresh each time.

Find a few good poems you enjoy and have them bookmarked for easy access. You can take the time to read one in combination with a tea ritual or by itself to redirect attention and connect with your feelings.

If you want to engage in this practice more deeply, you can read the poem aloud, or even read it to music and play with how to say it in the most impactful way for yourself, or you can memorize it for the fun of it. Engagement with spoken word can be a good entry into ecstatic poetry. If you would rather hear other people recite poetry, there are wonderful recordings readily available, some set to music, which are very beautiful and evocative.

Make a List

Start your day by making a list—not the definitive, prioritized to-do list, but rather a list of activities that you normally don't list, because you consider them mundane, a luxury, or because they fall into the category of self-care; in short, the things that tend to fall through the cracks. The trick here is to be realistic and not just aspirational. Adding things to your day that are not logistically possible just adds to the feeling of overwhelm. Pick one or two activities or rituals that can be easily done in five to ten minutes. Then list them among things you do anyway, but never consider to be part of your daily accomplishments.

This is a trick I have been using for many years and one that never fails me. I get up and make myself a cup of tea. Before I do anything else, I sit down in front of my copious to-do list (I still keep my lists on thick yellow pads, much more satisfying to me than their electronic counterparts, which I have to rely on while traveling). I get an overview of my day, then I make a short list for the first part of my day. Things that might go on this list:

- Get up
- Brush teeth
- Make tea
- Make list
- Have breakfast
- Check on plants and animals
- Movement practice
- New flowers on office altar

- Take vitamins
- Make grocery list
- Start workday

As you can see, many items are self-evident, but nonetheless, by the time I have written the list, I can check four or five items off as being completed. As much as this is a mind trick, it works in a few ways:

- It gives me a feeling of accomplishment for having done and checked off these things.
- It brings my attention to the many steps I do each day that I tend to discount.
- It brings mindfulness and attention to the mundane actions of the day, which keep me well and healthy.
- It provides a positive feedback system for the self-care and non-commerce-oriented aspects of my day.

On tough days, I might add a few positive affirmations to the list. Some examples are:

- "This is going to be an exciting day!" (Code for "Don't panic.")
- "By tonight I will know where to focus next." (Code for "Don't get overwhelmed.")
- "So much exciting new stuff!" (Code for "Don't get into a negative spiral of perceived overload.")

I tend to get a bit distracted and pulled in many directions in the morning, so this list is my go-to redirection tool. I don't start e-mails and work until this list is done, which allows me to incorporate self-care and body-oriented activities before I dive in to my workday.

8. Altars and Beauty

Altars are a wonderful way to engage with ritual, vision, and archetypal wisdom. And by "altars," I don't mean religious displays, but rather collections of items that are meaningful to you.

The act of putting together a tableau of items, spending time with them, and displaying them in a way that they can be seen and felt, is very powerful on many levels. From the beginning of time, we have displayed objects of beauty and power—from caves to cathedrals, from Grandma's family picture collection to elaborate Peruvian *retablos*—collecting, arranging, and displaying is part of our collective psyche.

I have an altar in every room. Each altar has a different purpose. In my bedroom, I have the whole top of a dresser with all the items that hold the most sentimental value to me, items that signify love, relationship, spiritual meaning, and magic. There is a beautiful Tibetan statue that signifies sacred union, a Viking knife my father gave me for protection, a small teapot from my grandmother, deer antlers I found in the woods, a hand painted picture of Kali, fresh flowers from my garden, stones and shells from my travels, some oracle cards I collected over the years, an owl feather, a small bag with wolf hair, and rose-scented candles. I always put jewelry on the altar and pictures or objects that feel important in that moment.

My writing shed has an area with pictures, statues, and colors that signify creativity and inspiration: a statue of Lakshmi, the goddess of beauty, a few colorings from my travels, feathers from my chickens, and beautiful pink glass candles. My studio holds Quan Yin, who signifies compassion, Shiva to represent the Divine Masculine, and Saraswati, who is the patron of the arts and music. The altar that changes the most is the one on my office desk. Every Monday morning, I rearrange the items; I might take some items away, and add some things that support what I am working on that week, or notes I received that have meaning to me, or sometimes even mail I need to handle that feels difficult. One of the two statues on my office altar is a small Nepalese statue of Ganesh, who is said to support business and remove obstacles. This statue was brought back from Nepal by my father, and every time I look at it, it reminds me of him and the adventurous, wonderful man he is. There is also a small dancing woman to remind me of what I am dedicated to. I keep a ceremonial knife with owl feathers on my desk under which I place the mail and notes I want to work with that week. I pick new flowers and start each workday by lighting a candle and taking a moment to review my lists (and of course, drink copious amounts of tea).

This is a deeply personal process and each woman must find her own way. Building an altar isn't just about collecting some statues or sticks of incense. Which items have special meaning for you? Which themes do you wish to express? Only you can know those things, and so the process of constructing your personal altar connects you to all of these deep parts of your wild nature.

An altar is a visual reminder or affirmation, as well as a way to bring beauty and meaning into everyday life. In my tradition, it is one of the ways to engage with the different attributes of life in the representation of each statue. Regardless of your spiritual or religious orientation, what you place on your altar is a 3-D affirmation and a calling in and keeping alive of what matters most to you. I often hear women say that they feel like they are leaving their feminine behind when they work, and this is a potent way to keep our feminine orientation alive, no matter what we are doing.

These days I travel more than I am home, and wherever I go, I set up a little travel altar. I bring a few small, meaningful items with me, and then add to them from the local environment. We often teach in Amsterdam, so I get to indulge in beautiful local flowers there. In Byron Bay, I might add shells I found on the beach, or driftwood and feathers. I buy postcards and add whatever jewelry I brought along. Often, I take a picture of these altars as a reminder of that moment in time.

In one of my workshops, the women were given clay and asked to make their own altar statue based on whatever issue or intention they were working on. It was a powerful and creative way to give life to an intention, surround it with beauty, and then speak about it.

Here are some of the ingredients you could use for an altar, but of course there are no limits to your creativity.

- Pictures of loved ones, places, inspirational figures, or teachers
- Statues or figurines that have meaning to you
- Postcards or notes you have received
- Written or drawn affirmations, prayers, or blessings
- Items of protection: salt, red string, evil-eye deterrents or a Hamsa, driftwood, stones, shells, and other natural items
- Bowls, plates, saucers, and ceramics
- Items that have spiritual significance to you
- Items of power
- Anything that holds beauty for you
- Candles and incense
- Flowers

Gathering items for your altar can be a process in itself. Begin by exploring what holds meaning and significance for you, what you want to remember, what you'd like to call in, and what is simply beautiful and inspiring to you.

Find a place to display these items and arrange them in a way that is pleasing to you. Then sit in front of your display and connect with each item. Feel its significance for you and enjoy what you have created. You can come back to connecting with it anytime you want to be reminded of your intention. Make sure that you add fresh flowers and light incense or candles to refresh and reconnect. And of course, you can always add and change things.

Another version of an altar would be a combination of a few objects that signify beauty to you. Find a small bud vase so you can display a single flower, and add an item or two to it. Or place a scented candle on your desk. Even if it's not lit, it will have enough fragrance to act as a reminder for your body. The key is to have items and areas that beckon you to come back to what is innately embodied and feminine in you. "Little and often" is much more effective than cutting yourself off all week and attending a "goddess retreat" on the weekend.

Lighting Candles and Intention-Setting

There are many ways to focus our minds. One effective strategy is to make positive affirmations. Much has been written on the subject, and the related advice goes from woo-woo to extremely practical.

I find it useful to write down a few key intentions before I start in the morning. I pick one affirmation for each area I'd like to cover that day: work, creativity, self-care, beauty, and movement.

You can create your own "menu" of topics you'd like to integrate into your day. Once again, it's about doability, not aspiration. Pick affirmations you can easily state and feel in your body, otherwise it's just magical thinking.

Phrase each affirmation in a way that feels positive and doable for you. Take a moment and write them all down. (I keep my affirmations with my lists for the day.) Read your affirmations aloud and light a candle or do some smudging as a way to engage with the process. It's useful to review your affirmations on occasion throughout the day.

9. Communion with Nature

Nothing brings us back to our natural flow like nature does. Find a place you can walk in, sit, swim, or just enjoy your surroundings. It doesn't matter whether your chosen place is by a tree in a local park or a beautiful beach. Being outdoors has many benefits, including health benefits from being in sunlight, regulation of blood pressure, and enhanced mood. Allow yourself to immerse your senses by being in a beautiful, natural environment, enjoying animal sounds, plant life, and a breeze on your skin.

Sitting and Looking Out

Find a place to sit comfortably in nature. Depending on where you live, this could be your garden, balcony, park, or a more untouched area of the woods or beach. For a moment, close your eyes. Feel where your body meets the surface you are sitting on, and feel downward from there into the ground. Let your imagination/vision travel further downward, as far as you can imagine, traveling down through layers of soil, gravel, stone, and water toward the core of the earth, and back up to where your body meets the ground. Then feel the air on your skin and let yourself feel upward through the clear sky, moving through layers of clouds, then imagine, as you rise, passing by an airplane, perhaps seeing people sitting and having drinks, then further out to the layers of stratosphere into open space, to encounter the moon, planets, stars, and galaxies.

From there, bring your attention to the sounds you can hear, noticing nature sounds, voices, traffic, airplanes, and the sounds of your own body and breathing.

Then open your eyes and "see out." Keeping your gaze somewhat wide and unfocused, notice how much you can see at once without focusing on one thing. Let your gaze wander and "just see." Now and again, bring your attention to what you can hear, to what your skin feels—perhaps a breeze or the warmth of the sun. Feel down into the earth and up into the sky, then come back to seeing. Let all the different sensations, sounds, and images function like a massage of your system. Do this for at least five minutes without fidgeting or getting distracted.

Water Practices

Immersing your body in water is one of the most profound ways to soften and calm your system. Saltwater has additional benefits, whether it's water from the ocean or from a good Epsom salt bath. One of my favorite quotes by Danish author Karen Blixen summarizes this very beautifully: "The cure for anything is saltwater—sweat, tears, or the sea."[19]

There are so many benefits to water immersion, even if the water is not saltwater. Our bodies are predominantly water. In elemental practice, it is said that because water can clean itself when it moves, the body moving in water is extremely cleansing and soothing for the nervous system.

Depending on your environment, you might choose to swim in a pool, lake, or ocean. If swimming is not your thing, you can immerse in a bathtub or have a shower as your water practice. If none of this can be done, you can just sit by water, or find a recording of water sounds.

Immerse in water and feel the temperature and texture, the subtle pressure of the water on your body. Move your body in ways that feel good and sensitize you to the effects of the water. Relax your muscles as much as possible, without going limp. Determine which muscles need to be active in this moment and which are just habitually tense. Imagine the water not only cleansing your skin, but also releasing all different aspects of you. Spend as much of your attention as you can on all aspects of the water immersion, all the way through emerging from the water and drying your body, attending to your body with cleansing and soothing in mind.

If you are sitting by the water or listening to water sounds, you can do this practice as a visualization and still receive benefits. Our body reacts to visualizations as if they are really happening, a phenomenon that high-performance sports athletes sometimes incorporate into their training.

Barefoot Walking

Find a place where you can walk barefoot safely and pleasurably. Begin by placing your bare feet on the ground and let yourself stand for a moment. Closing your eyes, feel how your feet make contact with the ground. Relax the soles of your feet and imagine that you are sinking into the surface of the ground. Notice your attention moving into the ground, and bring your center of gravity as low as possible. Then open your eyes and explore the texture of the ground visually. As you begin walking, set each foot down deliberately, feeling the varying texture of whatever ground you are on. Take your time just walking around. Notice how your body feels as you move, and imagine and feel your connection to the earth, as you connect your lower body with the ground on each step. At the end of this practice, sit or lie on the ground, letting yourself feel the pull of gravity as you relax your body downward.

Gardening—Getting Your Hands in the Dirt

In one of our women's study groups, I teach elemental practices. The first segment engages with earth, both literally and in subtle body explorations.

You can engage in this practice as well: Start by buying a packet of bean seeds. You can choose a bush or climbing variety, depending on the space you have. (Climbing beans are much more fun!) If you are planting in a pot, fill the pot with soil, moisten the soil thoroughly, and stick one seed in the middle, about half an inch deep. Keep it moist, put it close to a sunny window, and watch for the emerging sprout. If you are planting outside, make sure that your seed is protected and receives full sunlight.

Each time you engage with your seedling and, later on, plant, take a few minutes to look at the plant; notice the textures and colors, feel the moistness of the soil, inhale its scent, and watch the water sink into it. If you want to engage even more fully with the act of growing, you can take daily pictures or record the experience in a journal. Make sure to harvest and eat your beans!

The daily engagement with emerging life—the fragility of the seedling on one side and the robust determination of the plant to climb, grow, and fruit on the other—are beautiful metaphors for life, and often our participants draw conclusions about their general attitude toward life itself via the engagement with the bean plant.

Rudolf Steiner, the founder of biodynamic farming and my fellow countryman, suggested doing "plant meditations" to become more sensitive to life-force and nature. This practice is one way of doing so.

10. Animals

Engaging with animals is my favorite practice and my number one "feminine remembering" activity. I live on a small farm with many rescued animals and a pack of small, unruly dogs. No matter how much masculine activity I have to do, no matter how tight my neck and shoulders are after a few hundred e-mails, the moment I go and see my animals, everything resets, and I relax. Often, when I have deadlines or difficult office days, I'll take breaks periodically and check on my farm animals, or I'll cuddle one of the dogs. It's my version of "feminine hygiene," a constant remembering of my heart and body in the midst of a hectic day.

When we teach workshops at my studio, the participants get to enjoy life at the farm. They love when chickens or ducks waddle by, or the gigantic tortoise ambles across the lawn, or the donkeys bray to announce that they are hungry. Curly, one of my pigs, loves to hang around when I teach women's groups. We always thought she just wanted to be "one of the girls" until I realized at some point that she was just waiting for everyone to go back inside for their next session, so she could go through their purses and steal their chocolates and snacks.

My animals become an integral part of the retreat experience and provide a link between experiential learning activities and the land. They open hearts and provide fuzzy ears to touch, and beckon the connection to the natural world.

If you happen to have a pet, or have access to animals in some way, make some time to connect with them without distraction. Feel them and watch the way they behave. Touch them and feel the warmth of their bodies and the texture of their skin or coat. Feel them from your heart, imagining that your heart connects with theirs. You'll be amazed by the beautiful connection and communion that comes from there.

Compassion for animals, to me, is the practice for an embodied, heartfelt life. From there, the compassion can spread to other humans and to ourselves, as well as to nature and the environment. Often, it's not so easy to have compassion for our fellow human beings, who don't always agree with us. By feeling and loving an innocent animal, we train our "love and compassion" muscles, which in turn means we have greater love and compassion in all aspects of our life.

11. Creativity

Creativity is every woman's birthright. We are born to create, not only in the form of growing and birthing humans, but also in the form of providing, beautifying, and connecting. From singing lullabies to creating sustenance, we are always using our creative force. It might not be formal art, but we all have the ability to create.

The way we dress, how we create our environment, what we cook, how we create gatherings, and how we solve problems are all intricately connected to our creative life-force. You might not consider yourself artistic or creative, but most of what we do utilizes our creative ability. It does not matter what you do—conscious, active, creative engagement stimulates the body, mind, and soul, brings forth more creation, and supports problem-solving capacity.

Coloring
This is one of my favorite pastimes on long flights and when I want to unwind. There is a vast variety of coloring books to play with. The fun thing about coloring, to me, has to do with the fact that the outline provides the structure within which I can let myself go creatively. Since the structure is there, I can fill in the lines with every color and shading combination I am inspired to use. I often make several copies of my favorite coloring images and play with color schemes, and even add textures with sparkly pens, or glue on rhinestones or feathers. We use coloring in our advanced women's groups as a way to immerse with

archetypes, with each woman producing many variations of the same archetype. Those colorings are incredibly evocative and creative, and the women report that they serve as a kind of diary, reflecting the mood and circumstance of each practice session. I use my colorings on my travel altars and enjoy the play with textures and colors immensely.

Find a coloring book you enjoy (I have listed some of my favorites in the Resources section, p. 242) and buy some colored pencils. I recommend getting a relatively small set of good quality pencils and then picking up additional individual pencils in your favorite colors from the art supply store. That way, you get to play with a variety of your favorites instead of ending up with a lot of brown/beige/gray ones in a large set. Set some time aside to sit with the book and find an outline that calls to you. It's fun to do this with friends and see how each woman creates differently. Allow yourself to experiment with textures and colors you find pleasing, and suspend the need to do it perfectly. There is always another coloring page to play with.

Decorating

Find an area of your living space that has been neglected for a while, ideally a small, manageable area, to begin with. Look at the whole room, then the area you are playing with, and start imagining how you could freshen up this spot. It's always good to start with clearing away anything that does not need to be there and giving the area a cleaning. Then rearrange the area. Even if you are keeping it the same, arrange it freshly and feel what could be done to refresh the feeling. Once you are finished, take some time to enjoy your handiwork. Do this on occasion in different parts of your space and notice what happens as a result.

Make a Music Playlist

Revisit your music collection and create a few new playlists. Pick a few different moods and create music you can dance to, move with, or use as accompaniment for tea, oracle cards, coloring, or taking a bath. Create playlists to inform and inspire your body and mood. Play around with different emotions that come through the music and, if you have time, try finding new songs or past favorites. This is also a great project to share with a friend: exchanging music and playing your playlists for each other. Music evokes such depth of feeling and adds so much to our lives! I have whole playlists of songs I sing along to in the car, others for bumpy flights (not singing aloud there!), and some very specific collections for different practices.

Vision Board

In the past, I always rolled my eyes at vision boards and dismissed them as magical thinking. Then, when I bought my farm, I bought some interior design magazines to get inspiration. Before I would throw them out, I would often cut out pictures of animals, tables set in orchards, and roses climbing up barn doors. Eventually, I made these collections into two boards with photos I really loved and hung them on my office wall. There was a picture of a donkey under an apple tree that I really loved, and I remember thinking how lucky these people were to be able to own a donkey. A few years later, when I changed a few things around in my office, I realized that everything I had put on these two boards was now part of my house, including the donkey.

In hindsight, I realized that the pictures had informed my body-mind, and each time I looked at them, not only did I see things I desired, but more importantly, I felt happiness in seeing things I loved, which inspired and informed my daily life and decisions. In a round-about way, the things we see daily and the way things are organized around us inform our nervous system and our orientation, so why not create beauty and images that inspire us?

Since then, I have been collecting pictures as inspirations, and with the creation of Pinterest, I now keep elaborate mood and vision boards electronically as well. I do believe that seeing them often, even without being aware of them, helps to get the information they convey into the subconscious mind.

Learn Something New and Change Things Up

Learning a new skill creates confusion and takes us out of our rote habits. Being on autopilot and doing whatever we know how to do is comforting and takes less energy, but it also makes us less and less sensitive, awake, and curious. When we learn something new, our system has to adjust. With that, things get shaken up. We might feel agitation or discomfort, or even get discouraged. The saying "You can't teach an old dog a new trick" might come to mind, and we might give up. (Take heart, the saying is wrong. Dogs learn fine until the very end.) The benefits of new skill development for creativity and awareness are immense. Even if you don't have the time or resources to learn something new, change up your routines. There are simple ways to do this. Drive a different route to work or school, brush your teeth with your nondominant hand, and—*shudder*—turn your toilet paper roll the other way around. See if you can get out of the autopilot mode and allow your body and mind to access different pathways.

12. Sensuality Hacks

Even on the busiest day, we can take small actions to care for ourselves and our bodies. Every time we touch base with these small activities, our body remembers, and over time, we stay more sensually alive and embodied.

Here are some of my tried-and-true go-to's:

Rosewater Mist

Danny, my wonderful facialist, makes an incredibly fragrant rosewater mist that I carry with me everywhere. Just a few mists in the midst of whatever intense activity I am engaged in brings me, literally, back to my senses. Spray the mist toward your face, inhale, and savor the scent.

Apply Hand Cream

I carry a small tin of hand cream with me so I can massage my hands while I am on the phone, on a plane, or anywhere else I can fit in a few minutes. Just touching and pressing my hands brings me back to feeling my body.

Essential Oils

A very quick reset, and also effective when you feel tired. Put a few drops of essential oil into your palm, rub your hands together, and inhale the scent by bringing your palms to your nose. I love rose oil and ylang-ylang, and as well as an oil made by Young Living called Thieves, which I use when I feel like I am getting sick.

Have your Favorite Tea in a Thermos

My teaching partner, Steve, travels with a gigantic thermos, which we fill with peppermint tea each morning when we are on the road. All day while we teach, we can enjoy the fresh, clean taste of hot peppermint tea. Each time he pours a cup, I get to inhale the fragrant steam, and with each cup, I enjoy a feeling of well-being, a sense of ritual, and the invigorating taste of mint.

Carry Something Pleasing to Touch

Ever since I was a child, I have collected chestnuts and round stones and carried them in my pockets. Touching the smooth, round surface provides instant connection to my sensory system and often brings the memory of where I found the specific stone or chestnut, adding a nice emotional note to the experience.

Foot Massage Ball under the Desk

This is one of my newest go-to's, which I use while doing computer work. I have a little prickly foot massage ball under my desk. When I notice that I have lost track of my body's sensations and my neck and shoulders have started hurting, I roll the ball underneath my bare feet, which reinvigorates my access to sensation. My attention is drawn down out of my head and into my body, and aliveness begins to return.

V

Closing

you will become a graveyard
of all the women you once were
before you rise one morning
embraced by your own skin.

you will swallow
a thousand different names
before you taste the meaning
held within your own.[20]

This poem by the gifted young poetess Pavana Reddy beautifully speaks of my wish for you. May this book support you in connecting to your very own Wild Way. May your enlivened body guide you to embrace who you truly are. And may your untamed heart love with abandon.

Acknowledgments

I HAVE BEEN IMMENSELY FORTUNATE TO BE BORN TO TRULY INCREDIBLE parents. Deep gratitude to Ulrich and Sylvia, whose sanity, love, and generosity have informed my life to a great extent. Their outlook and disposition have allowed me to follow my path, equipped with a knowledge of love and discipline, and equal curiosity and sensibility. Their marriage, still going strong and beautifully alive, has informed much of my personal and professional inquiry on what makes a relationship function. Their acceptance of my "weird" interests and willingness to support me has shaped my path to this day. My gratitude to my sister Birgit and my nieces Isabel and Lilliana for continuing the female "Boehm Lineage."

Deepest gratitude to Steve James, my teaching, creative, and business partner and dear friend, without whom this book would never have happened. Your vision, direction, and contributions have been invaluable to me in bringing the lineage forward. Our friendship inspires me and makes traveling and teaching a great adventure.

I could not function on such a high-performance, high-travel level without the help of the amazing women who support me: Casey Carey, who manages our whole operation, connects with our students, and, during the writing of this book, single-handedly managed my work life. Siena di Francesco, who tirelessly, competently, and gracefully provides support during teaching, and whose beautiful heart greets and supports anyone coming to a workshop in Ojai. Danny Neifert, who helps and supports our teaching in Ojai and, in her professional life, provides me with incredible facials and skin care. Dawn Matlock, who is like a fairy godmother, both to me and to my animals, caring twice a day, every day, for my motley crew of rescues, loving them as if they were her own. Without her I would not be able to leave knowing that everyone is well-loved and cared for. Caitlin Mathews, whose expert chiropractic care and uncanny intuition keep my body aligned and my field clear throughout all my travels. Nelly Rubiano, who unfailingly brings the ranch back to order and cleanliness, no matter how many dogs, workshop participants, or guests come through.

To my incredible clients, who inspire me to stay on top of my game in order to support them well, thank you. My special thanks to Will and Chris, whose care and support have been beyond incredible. To our students and, especially, the women's and men's groups in Ojai and Amsterdam, your active participation and ongoing practice is inspiring. Many thanks to Nyei Murez for her calm, competent support of reading and editing during the writing of this book. Zhena Muzyka, my editor and publisher, you are a force of nature and an inspiration; I am so grateful to be part of your Enliven family.

To Rod Thompson, who is a true man of God, thank you for being such a steadfast resource, support, and example. Michael Ellsberg, for your friendship and being a cheerleader for my writing. Oliver and Sophie Butcher, you are the best neighbors anyone could ever wish for. John Halford, and Nikki, who is both a friend and my incredible veterinarian, whom I can count on for help no matter the time of day. To the late James Baye, my love and gratitude for our adventures together in life and death. To Magdalena, with thanks for your wisdom and knowledge. And finally, my deepest gratitude to my teacher, the late Deepa, for giving me her knowledge, her practice, and her lineage.

Resources

Michaela's Workshops, Trainings, and Events
www.michaelaboehm.com

Michaela's Lectures on SoundCloud
Sixty-plus hours of free lectures and content: www.soundcloud.com
/michaela-boehm.

Movement and Embodiment

The Non-Linear Movement Method®
For training and classes visit: www.thenonlinearmovementmethod.com.

Movement Koan® Method
Steve James's Movement Koan® is a fusion of joint-nourishing movement and body-based mindfulness. It's a great means of engaging with
the body in a gentle, effective way: www.guruviking.com.

5 Rhythms®
The work of Gabrielle Roth. A dynamic dance practice facilitating
connection with the body: www.5rhythms.com.

Somatic Experiencing/Trauma Healing
The work of Dr. Peter A. Levine. The site includes an international
practitioner directory: www.traumahealing.org.

Meditation and Resources for Applied Practice
Steve James offers a unique blend of practices, education, and insight:
www.guruviking.com.

Poetry

Pavana Reddy writes beautiful, evocative poetry for women:
www.pavanareddy.com.

Altarpieces, Incense, and Ritual Supplies

The Bodhi Tree carries a beautiful variety of statues, pictures, incense,
and smudging supplies, as well as crystals, cards, and ritual supplies:
www.bodhitree.com.

The Shaman's Market offers my favorite Palo Santo incense, plus
essential oils, statues, rattles, and supplies to create sacred space.
www.shamansmarket.com.

Oracle Cards

The Wild Unknown: Kim Krans is an incredible illustrator and has
created two beautiful card decks: www.thewildunknown.com.

Coloring Books

Ekabhumi Charles Ellik is a gifted artist who created my all-time favorite
coloring books: *The Shakti Coloring Book: Goddesses, Mandalas, and
the Power of Sacred Geometry* and *The Bhakti Coloring Book: Deities,
Mandalas, and the Art of Playful Meditation*: www.ekabhumi.com.

Recommended Reading

Altars: Bringing Sacred Shrines into Your Everyday Life by Denise Linn

*In an Unspoken Voice: How the Body Releases Trauma and Restores Good-
ness* by Peter A. Levine, Ph.D.

The Radiance Sutras: 112 Gateways to the Yoga of Wonder and Delight by
Lorin Roche PhD: www.radiancesutras.com.

*Sweat Your Prayers: The Five Rhythms of the Soul—Movement as Spiri-
tual Practice* by Gabrielle Roth

Bibliography

Bradley, Marion Zimmer. *The Mists of Avalon*. New York: Alred A. Knopf, 1982.

Jung, Carl. *C. G. Jung: The Collected Works of C. G. Jung*. New York: Routledge, 2014.

Levine, Peter A., PhD. *In an Unspoken Voice: How the Body Releases Trauma and Restores Goodness*. Berkeley, California: North Atlantic Press, 2010.

_____. *Healing Trauma: A Pioneering Program for Restoring the Wisdom of Your Body*. Boulder, Colorado: Sounds True, 2008.

Linn, Denise. *Altars: Bringing Sacred Shrines into Your Everyday Life*. Wellspring/Ballantine, 1999.

Reddy, Pavana. *Rangoli*. USA: CreateSpace Independent Publishing Platform, 2017.

Roche, Lorin, PhD. *The Radiance Sutras*. Boulder, Colorado: Sounds True, 2014.

Roth, Gabrielle. *Sweat Your Prayers: The Five Rhythms of the Soul—Movement as Spiritual Practice*. New York: TarcherPutnam, 1998.

Van der Kolk, Bessel. *The Body Keeps the Score: Brain, Mind, and Body in the Healing of Trauma*. New York: Penguin, 2015.

Weldon, Fay. *The Life and Loves of a She Devil*. Great Britain: Hodder and Stoughton, 1983.

Notes

1   C. G. Jung, *C. G. Jung: The Collected Works* (New York: Routledge, 2014) 7214.

2   Gloria Feldt, as quoted in "Beyond the Bedroom: What the Birth Control Pill Really Did for Women," by Hannah Seligson, *Forbes,* May 12, 2010, https://www.forbes.com/2010/05/12/sexual-revolution-planned-parenthood-unplanned-pregnancy-forbes-woman-health-birth-control-pill.html.

3   Ibid.

4   Gabrielle Roth, *Sweat Your Prayers: The Five Rhythms of the Soul—Movement as Spiritual Practice* (New York: TarcherPutnam, 1998).

5   Peter A. Levine, PhD, *In an Unspoken Voice: How the Body Releases Trauma and Restores Goodness* (Berkeley, California: North Atlantic Press, 2010).

6   Peter A. Levine, PhD, *Healing Trauma: A Pioneering Program for Restoring the Wisdom of Your Body* (Boulder, Colorado: Sounds True, 2008), 32.

7   Isabel Allende, "TED Talk: How to Live Passionately—No Matter Your Age," filmed March 2014 at TED2014, Vancouver, Canada, video, 8:17, https://www.ted.com/talks/isabel_allende_how_to_live_passionately_no_matter_your_age.

8   Ibid.

9   Katherine Crowley and Kathi Elster, *Mean Girls at Work: How to Stay Professional When Things Get Personal* (New York: McGraw-Hill, 2012).

10 Meredith Fuller, *Working with Bitches: Identify the Eight Types of Office Mean Girls and Rise Above Workplace Nastiness* (Boston: Da Capo Press, 2013).

11 Susan Shapiro Barash, *Tripping the Prom Queen: The Truth About Women and Rivalry,* (New York: St. Martin's Press, 2006).

12 Jordan B. Peterson, PhD, speaking in "2017/02/11: An Incendiary Discussion at Ryerson U," https://www.youtube.com/watch?v=8ABa4RdNPxU, March 2017.

13 Ibid.

14 Fay Weldon, speaking in "Fay Weldon: What Her Generation of Feminists Got Wrong—*BBC Newsnight,*" https://www.youtube.com/watch?v=WvrsRnrH-i0&list=FL5CDoXRwxZpeKlfsZlcjPhw&index=31, April 2017.

15 Peterson, "An Incendiary Discussion."

16 Weldon, "Generation of Feminists."

17 Peterson, "An Incendiary Discussion."

18 Traditional smudging prayer, source unknown.

19 Karen Blixen (Isak Dinesen), as quoted in *Reader's Digest,* April 1964.

20 Pavana Reddy, "You Will Become a Graveyard," *Rangoli.* USA: CreateSpace Independent Publishing Platform, 2017.

About the Author

Michaela Boehm is a relationship and embodiment expert who has taught workshops and reached clients around the world for more than twenty-five years. Born and raised in Austria, Michaela combines her Jungian training and extensive clinical counseling experience with her in-depth training in the yogic arts.

Michaela empowers her students through an eclectic mix of education, experiential exercises, and guided explorations. Known for her work with high-performing individuals, she counts among her ongoing clients Academy Award–winning actors, business pioneers, and multiple Grammy Award–winning musicians, including Will Smith and Gwyneth Paltrow. Michaela lives on an organic farm in California, where she rescues and rehabilitates animals. For more information, please visit her website at MichaelaBoehm.com.